AMERICAN
HERITAGE

April, 1968 · Volume XIX, Number 3

About History: A Horse of a Different Color

Cantering up on his white charger, Washington stared at Lee with an expression so wrathful that few of his aides would ever forget it.

"What is the meaning of this, Sir?" the red-faced commander-in-chief demanded.

Lee turned his glance aside and began to mutter something none of the witnesses could quite make out. Before he had finished, Washington whipped out his sword, waved it aloft, and with a violent curse, shouted to the retreating American troops to stand and fight. The rout was stemmed.

So reads one description of the dramatic climax of the Battle of Monmouth on June 28, 1778. How true is it?

That question—How true is it?—is one that bothers the editors of this magazine all the time. From the beginning, we have promised our readers history that will be both lively and accurate. We have stubbornly eschewed historical fiction, whether it be invented dialogue, colorful details without factual foundation, or episodes wholly devised by an imaginative contributor. We are committed to telling the truth about the past—yet if there is one motto emblazoned on our editorial ensign it is that good history should make the past come alive. We like the way it was put by a nineteenth-century American historian named James Handasyd Perkins:

I may listen with infinite tedium to one man's account of a merry meeting, or a pitched battle, for he will but give me the fact that men and women laughed, and danced, or that two parties fell to and fought; while to another, who shall paint me the very men and women, and how this one was dressed, and that one held her head, and the other stepped off with a partner having a cork leg, or who shall make me see the red-coated soldiers, and hear the swearing sergeants, and watch the cool yeomanry, holding their fire till they see the white of their enemies' eyes—to this man I could listen if I had not slept for forty-eight hours.

The trouble is, of course, that when all is said and done the past is irretrievable. What happened to you yesterday? Nobody can give more than a faltering and partial account of his own recent past. The ordinary moments are swept indifferently into history by the second hand on the clock, and even as they go, a haze of uncertainty rises around them. It grows denser as time goes by. As for the extraordinary moments—the surprising, disappointing, terrifying, or ecstatic moments that we will "never forget"—they are so meaningful to us that out of them we build our personal myths, and in a few weeks or months or years we no longer know what really happened; we only know how we tell the story.

This human bias is damnably apt

The man on the white horse . . . . .

to affect historians, too, and the best of them have always been skeptically aware of it. Herodotus, the father of history, liberally salted the opening chapter of his *Persian Wars* with "according to the Greeks" and "according to the Persians"; and a modern wit, brooding perhaps on that, came up with "One man's Mede is another man's Persian." Henry Steele Commager argued in our pages not long ago that ideally the historian should not make moral judgments on the behavior of earlier generations; but he

recognized that such detachment is almost beyond human capacity. The scholar who can write well of the American or French or Russian Revolution without caring who won has yet to appear. Meanwhile, historians continue to give accounts of past events that veer toward their own prejudices, and this doesn't do much to burn off the fog enveloping "what really happened."

Truly, the task of the historian sometimes looks hopeless—yet it is a most vital human enterprise, and one we are all engaged in whether we know it or not. For the only thing that lets us make sense out of our experience, personal or communal, is that, broadly speaking, history does repeat itself. The future is just a guess; the present instant, taken alone, is as meaningless as a single note isolated from a fugue. Time flows continuously into the past, and if there is any distinguishable pattern, we can see it only by looking backward. It is when we contemplate the past, and adjust our anticipation of the future accordingly, that we live as human beings.

So we are all historians. One consequence is that there are many different approaches, in art and science as well as in history proper, to making sense out of the past. We can be thankful that, before photography, most painters were not abstractionists but did their best to show things just as they appeared. Many diaries and journals occupy a fertile middle ground between literature and history; even the line between history and fiction is not always easy to draw. Henry Fielding unabashedly called his extravagant novel *The History of Tom Jones, a Foundling,* and there can be no doubt that it brilliantly illuminates for us the eighteenth-century English scene. Everybody knows what truth is stranger than, but it may be—so claim the artists—that fiction is sometimes truer than truth. Matthew Arnold spoke sourly of "that huge Mississippi of falsehood called History," and if "truth" *is* stranger than

AMERICAN HERITAGE

The Magazine of History

SENIOR EDITOR
Bruce Catton

EDITOR
Oliver Jensen

MANAGING EDITOR
Robert Lincoln Reynolds

ART DIRECTOR
Murray Belsky

ART EDITOR
Joan Paterson Kerr

ARTICLES EDITOR
E. M. Halliday

ASSOCIATE EDITORS
Robert S. Gallagher   David G. Lowe
Barbara Klaw   John L. Phillips
Douglas Tunstell

COPY EDITOR
Brenda Niemand

EDITORIAL ASSISTANTS
Mary Dawn Earley   Rosemary L. Klein
Mary A. Hawkins   Joanne Shapiro

PUBLISHER
Darby Perry

ADVISORY BOARD
Allan Nevins, *Chairman*
Carl Carmer   Louis C. Jones
Gerald Carson   Alvin M. Josephy, Jr.
Marshall B. Davidson   Howard H. Peckham
John A. Garraty   Francis S. Ronalds
Eric F. Goldman   S. K. Stevens

AMERICAN HERITAGE is published every two
months by American Heritage Publishing Co.,
Inc., 551 Fifth Avenue, New York, N.Y. 10017.

PRESIDENT
James Parton

CHAIRMAN, EDITORIAL COMMITTEE
Joseph J. Thorndike

MANAGING DIRECTOR, BOOK DIVISION
Richard M. Ketchum

SENIOR ART DIRECTOR
Irwin Glusker

Correspondence about subscriptions should be
sent to: American Heritage Subscription Office, 383 West Center Street, Marion, Ohio
43302. Single copies: $4.25. Annual subscrip-
tions: $16.50 in U.S. and Canada; $17.50 elsewhere. An annual Index of AMERICAN HERI-
TAGE is published in February, priced at $1.00.
AMERICAN HERITAGE will consider but assumes
no responsibility for unsolicited materials.
Title registered U.S. Patent Office. Second-
class postage paid at New York, N.Y., and
at additional mailing offices.

Sponsored by

American Association for State & Local History · Society of American Historians

CONTENTS *April, 1968 · Volume XIX, Number 3*

COVER: The full name might have been Michael Walter Disney Mouse, for the rather bumptious little creature was in many ways an alter ego of his famous creator. It was Walt Disney's voice that was heard as Mickey's after the talkies arrived in 1928, and it can be argued that a subtle evolution in Mickey's character, over the years, reflected Disney's effort to improve his own public image. These and other absorbing matters are examined in a new book on the Disney empire by Richard Schickel; an excerpt from it begins on page 24. Our cover shows Mickey Mouse in the first effulgence of success in the thirties —amply fed, surrounded by trophies and status symbols like books and statues, thoroughly aware of himself as a figure of world renown. It was a Disney publicity release and comes to us from Culver Pictures. *Back Cover:* What the gentleman cyclist wore in 1884—shown here in an advertising lithograph owned by the Old Print Shop—was so groovy that we fully expect it to start another modern trend, perhaps even including the high-rise bicycles.

Fanny Kemble should have known that a beautiful, brilliant, vivacious British actress never, never marries the Butler—especially an American slave-holding Butler with a narrow vision of a wife's role

A Woman's Place

By JANET STEVENSON

Frances Anne Kemble, portrayed by Henry Inman as a Philadelphia matron, alternately shocked and angered the Butlers with her mercurial imagination and tenacious morality.

One June evening in 1834, Fanny Kemble, then the most popular actress in the English-speaking world, played her farewell performance in the Park Theatre in New York City. As the final curtain fell and the cast came out to take their bows, a young man who had been playing flute in the orchestra jumped to the stage and took Fanny's hand in a gesture that said as plainly as speech, "I take this woman for my wife."

That was the symbolic ceremony. The actual one had taken place a fortnight earlier, when Philadelphia society gathered in Christ Church to hear Miss Kemble and Pierce Mease Butler exchange vows. It was like the classic fairy tale ending in which the prince—young, handsome, and wealthy—carries off the princess to live happily ever after. As at all such events, there were a few voices of dissent and croaks of doom that went almost unheard at the time but that were to prove prophetic.

There was, for example, the editor of the Germantown *Telegraph,* who wrote: "He who weds her for an angel will discover, we opine, ere a fortnight that she is nothing more or less than a woman, and perhaps one of the most troublesome kind in the bargain." And there was Catharine Maria Sedgwick, the novelist, who considered Fanny "one of those rare beings through whom the Creator reminds us of the infinite perfectibility of man." Miss Sedgwick took a dim view of Pierce as a mate for a "most captivating creature, steeped to the lips with genius" because, although she had seen marriages between brilliant men and quite stupid women turn out well, she had not seen it work the other way around. And even among the young couple's most fervent well-wishers there was a nagging question as to why the most brilliant, original actress of her day should turn her back on the calling that had raised her family from obscurity to be intimates of the aristocracy of blood and brains in England, and seek fulfillment in the role of an American wife and mother, for which nothing had in any way prepared her.

The answer, in its simplest form, was that Fanny was leaving the stage because she hated it.

Although—or, perhaps, because—she was born into the royal family of the British theatre, the profession had never held any glamour for her. By the time she was old enough to know her aunt Sarah Siddons, the Tragic Muse was a pitiable old relic. Fanny's uncle, the great John Philip Kemble, was driven into bankruptcy and exile during her childhood by the burden of the royal license to produce plays in that great barn of a theatre, Covent Garden. Charles Kemble, Fanny's father, took over the license and the debts, and soon he was in the same dismal predicament. The Covent Garden jinx—or, as Fanny imagined it, the Minotaur

who dwelt in the great white marble maze—had played havoc with the health and happiness of the Kembles throughout Fanny's twenty years of life, but at least she had been assured that she would never be sacrificed to it.

Then one day, when the fortunes of the Theatre Royal Company seemed about to flounder into final catastrophe, Charles asked Fanny if she would read the part of Juliet for him, alone on the empty stage. She did, and, satisfied that her voice would carry to the last of the galleries, he proposed that she make her debut in that role in three weeks.

The announcement of a new Kemble debut would draw a crowd because the London world would be

Pierce Butler pursued the woman of his dreams with a verve and an enthusiasm he lacked as a husband.

looking for a second coming of the divine Sarah. Fanny was the only possible debutante. She was endowed with the Kemble voice, a dancer's grace (inherited from her mother), and a face that could project the entire range of human emotions. That Fanny's natural bent was for something as untheatrical as the study of moral philosophy was irrelevant in this crisis. She loved Shakespeare, spoke his verse intelligently, and had a remarkable facility for committing it to memory.

Was she willing to make the attempt?

She was not, but she was unwilling to refuse. She was

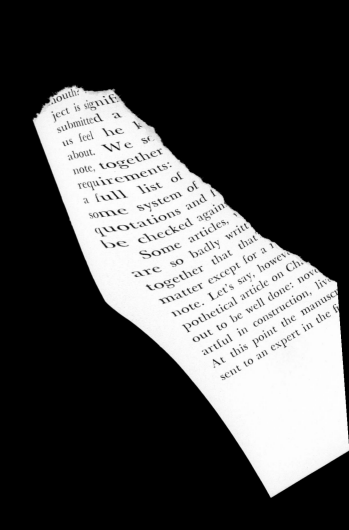

certain that she could not succeed at so impossible a task, but if her father's last hope depended on it, she would do as he asked. She began to rehearse with the company (which included her father as Mercutio and her mother as Lady Capulet), while bills announcing her first performance were posted all over London.

The gala audience that assembled to witness the event, on October 5, 1829, included the aging Sarah herself. The spectators could look from the stage to Mrs. Siddons' box and back. Fanny's first entrance was halting, her first lines spoken in a nervous, hushed voice. But suddenly people saw—or believed that they saw—the divine spark flash across the dark space and rekindle itself in a new human form. A miracle had happened. Fanny was not a second Sarah Siddons, but she was something just as enthralling. The London

theatre had a new divinity. Covent Garden, the Theatre Royal Company, and Charles Kemble's finances were saved.

But Fanny was trapped. Like Ariel, she was bound to serve out her term at tasks that might have seemed light or pleasant to another but were onerous to her. She was subjected to a glare of publicity and adulation that robbed her of most of the advantages of her success and added other strains to the physical and emotional ordeal of performing three or four times each week.

Fashionable portraitists like Sir Thomas Lawrence asked her to sit, and before long, cheap reproductions of her face were displayed on plates, scarves, and snuff boxes in the windows of London shops. Young gallants lined up outside the stage door to cheer her as she

*Charles Kemble posed in costume
for artist Thomas Sully in 1833.*

The Kemble Troupe

*England's acting royalty, the Kemble
family, dominate the trial of Queen
Katharine in G. H. Harlow's painting
of a scene from Shakespeare's* Henry
VIII. *The immortal Sarah Siddons, as
Katharine, gestures toward her brother,
the great John Philip Kemble, appear-
ing as Cardinal Wolsey. Fanny's father,
Charles Kemble, pen in hand, is Crom-
well, and directly behind him, as King
Henry, is his brother Stephen. One of
Fanny's cousins was cast in the role of
the page, with her back to the artist.*

Thomas Gainsborough painted the Tragic Muse, Sarah Siddons, in 1784.

emerged (always carefully chaperoned). Her brother's Cambridge cronies—brilliant young men like Will Thackeray, Alfred Tennyson, Richard Milnes, and Arthur Hallam—who had yesterday enjoyed matching wits with "John's little sister, Fan," were now too awed to approach her. She was a favorite guest at the great country houses of England and was sought out and made much of by the wisest and wittiest folk of the realm. But there was no time for resting or reading or riding—or falling in love. Her Prospero could not afford to be without her services even for a summer.

The problem was as simple as arithmetic. Covent Garden was solvent when Fanny played, insolvent when she did not. It took a full house every night to make any substantial profit. A bad week could wipe out the gains of a good month. So Fanny had to play as often as possible—all the first season, then a provincial tour; all the second season, then another tour.

She had been promised her freedom at the end of her third season, but as the time approached, the Covent Garden jinx stirred and struck.

Cholera swept through the London slums and thinned the crowds in the galleries. The fight over the Reform Bill sent the upper classes into the galleries of Parliament for their evening entertainment. To make matters worse, a series of lawsuits was pending in the courts against Covent Garden. Charles Kemble's health broke as the inevitable catastrophe became obvious, and for a while it looked as if the Minotaur were going to take away his life as well as his living.

When he recovered, he was forced to beg Fanny's help again. The Covent Garden license was gone, but he had debts to pay and the future to secure for himself and his wife, and for Fanny's younger siblings. There was only one way he could see to amass the ten thousand pounds he needed: a tour of the American "provinces." If such a venture succeeded at all, the money could be earned in a relatively short time. With Fanny he could do better than he could alone. It was, of course, hers to decide. . . .

Fanny knew that he could not succeed at all without her. Charles had become, as one unkind wit put it, "a great actor of minor parts." She could no more take responsibility for killing his last hope now than she could have three years ago. So she agreed, but only for two years. When she sailed for America, she felt that she was cutting herself off from everything and everyone she loved.

As Charles had foreseen, Fanny was the same sudden, stunning success that she had been in England. American audiences had seen some fine actors, but no actresses of Fanny's caliber. They were overwhelmed. Kemble performances (even with Charles playing Romeo to his daughter's Juliet) were consistently sold out. The Kembles were treated by officialdom with almost ceremonial respect, and by fashionable hostesses with boundless cordiality. Eligible bachelors from Boston to Washington, D.C., fell in love with Fanny at first sight, and envious debutantes paid her the ultimate compliment of copying her clothes.

Fanny was happy about the box-office receipts, but not about much else. She wrote home to a friend:

We are earning money very fast, and though I think we work too incessantly and too hard, yet, as every night we do not act is a certain loss of so much out of my father's pocket, I do not like to make many objections to it. . . . We rush from place to place, at each place have to drill a new set of actors, and every night to act a different play; so that my days are passed in dawdling about cold stages, with blundering actors who have not even had the conscience to study the words of their parts. . . . All the afternoon I pin up ribbons and feathers and flowers, and sort out theatrical adornments, and all the evening I enchant audiences, prompt my fellow mimes, and wish it had pleased Heaven to make me a cabbage in . . . a Christian kitchen-garden. . . .

Even before the first season was over, she felt her "sense exhausted, with looking, hearing, feeling, going, doing, being, and suffering." But she did her best to hide her discomfort and homesickness from her father until, halfway through her second season, the Sisyphus stone she had been pushing uphill all this time rolled back and crushed her.

Charles was in financial difficulties again, partly because of defaulting theatrical managers, partly because of the problems Mr. Biddle's United States Bank, in which he had deposited all of his savings, was having with President Jackson. It now appeared as if it would take yet another American season to earn the ten thousand pounds.

For the first—and perhaps the last—time in her life, Fanny felt unequal to the task. She went on for a few weeks and then suddenly accepted the most persistent of her suitors, a man who was able and eager to support her in what passed for luxury in the United States at that time. She could give all her savings to her father and send him home solvent, if not permanently secure. With that in mind, she announced her imminent retirement from the stage.

For a conventional man, young Mr. Butler had been wooing Fanny in a most unconventional fashion, following the Kembles from city to city, playing flute in the orchestra every night Fanny performed, and outlasting or outmaneuvering all his rivals, including the redoubtable Edward Trelawny, Byron's and Shelley's friend. But he did not intend to continue the romantic charade now that he had won the prize. What he looked forward to, it is clear from what he wrote and

William Thackeray   *Felix Mendelssohn*

Edward Trelawny   *William E. Channing*

A Star's Galaxy

Fanny's circle of intimates included many of the "greats" of the English-speaking world over a span of three quarters of a century. Thackeray, her brother's college chum, was a lifelong friend and admirer. Mendelssohn knew her as a fellow guest at parties in great English country houses, where he sometimes played his *Midsummer Night's Dream* music as background to Fanny's reading of the play. Trelawny, who had snatched Shelley's heart from the funeral pyre, failed after a vigorous courtship to win Fanny's. Channing, the Unitarian saint, talked with her at length about the abolition of slavery. Irving urged her on the eve of her marriage to "begin another and a brighter course with matured powers." Sully, the Philadelphia portraitist, befriended her during the early years of her stormy marriage. Sumner, the abolitionist senator, was her friend and unofficial marriage counselor. The Brownings knew and loved her as part of the expatriate society in Rome. Choate defended her in the sensational divorce action. Wister, author of *The Virginian,* had the benefit of his grandmother's literary criticism from an early age. James was her young escort in London when Fanny Kemble Butler was an aged but glamourous *grande dame.*

ALL PICTURES: CULVER

Washington Irving   *Thomas Sully*

Charles Sumner   *Rufus Choate*

Robert Browning   *Elizabeth Browning*

Owen Wister   *Henry James*

said later, was a life of domestic peace and the enjoyment of what society was offered in the small, smug world of Philadelphia's upper class. He was deeply in love with Fanny, and he seems really to have believed she would grace his world as she had graced the world she was giving up. He knew he was envied by thousands of men in England and America, and he felt himself fortunate beyond his deserts.

Fanny was not very much in love. One of her complaints against her profession was that "the constant simulation of emotion in time destroyed in itself the possibility of natural feeling." Besides, she was too

tired to feel much of anything but self-pity. But she was determined to make a good wife to Pierce, as she understood that role, and a good mother to the children she hoped to bear.

What she hoped for herself—besides the release from involuntary servitude—was a life of leisure in which to cultivate the neglected garden of her mind. She planned to take up her music again, to read, to think, and to write. Washington Irving had said to her, "You are acquiring materials and heaping together observations and experience and wisdom, and by and by, when . . . [you] retire from these labors, you will begin

CONTINUED ON PAGE 96

11

The "Military Crimes

The President, Members and Judge Advocate being sworn: The Judge Advocate prosecuting in the name of the United States of America, the Court proceed to the trial of Major-General Lee, who appears before the Court, and the following charges are exhibited against him:

First: For disobedience of orders, in not attacking the enemy on the 28th of June, agreeable to repeated instructions.

Secondly: For misbehaviour before the enemy on the same day, making an unnecessary, disorderly and shameful retreat.

Thirdly: For disrespect to the Commander-in-Chief, in two letters dated the 1st of July and the 28th of June.

The date was July 4, 1778. In the fields outside New Brunswick, New Jersey, the Continental Army of the United States of America was celebrating the second anniversary of the Declaration of Independence, but the atmosphere in the large room of Widow Voorhees' White Hart Tavern was anything but jolly. A stern major general, four grim-eyed brigadier generals, and eight solemn colonels heard these devastating accusations against a man who a short week before was widely considered, by both friend and foe, the most brilliant soldier in the American army. Major General Charles Lee was second in rank only to George Washington. In more modern terms, the situation could perhaps be paralleled by George Marshall's court-martialling Dwight Eisenhower at the height of World War II or Ulysses Grant's bringing charges against William Tecumseh Sherman on the eve of his march through Georgia. Either of these imaginary events would have won major historical attention. Yet the court-martial of Charles Lee has been strangely forgotten.

From the vantage of the comfortable historical privilege of hindsight, it is easy to say that a clash between Charles Lee and George Washington was inevitable. Temperamentally they were opposites. Washington made a habit of saying as little as possible; he had no

Emanuel Leutze's "study" of Washington at Monmouth contra[

f Charles Lee

By THOMAS J. FLEMING

en a major general was court-martialled

s at stake: George Washington's prestige

KIRBY COLLECTION, LAFAYETTE COLLEGE

ly with the canvas he did later on the same subject (see page 3).

pretensions to being either an intellectual or a military genius. Lee never stopped talking and considered himself—with some justification—both a military and a political theorist of the first rank. Though he could relax with intimates, Washington, like most conservatives, valued dignity and decorum. Lee valued neither. His uniform was invariably slovenly, and his conversation was sprinkled with phrases that made gentlemen wince and ladies blush. His constant company was a pack of dogs who shared his table, his bed, and his headquarters. Compounding these idiosyncrasies was an astonishing physical ugliness. He was thin and reedy, and his hands and feet were unusually small. His face was lean, dark, and bony, with an underslung jaw and a nose so long that for a time he was nicknamed Naso.

Yet this self-confessed eccentric dazzled a number of Americans when he arrived in the restless colonies in 1773 and immediately made it clear that he was heart and soul with the revolutionary cause. His credentials were impressive. He knew America, having fought with distinction as an officer in the 44th Regiment during the French and Indian War (he was adopted by the Mohawks, who nicknamed him Boiling Water). With British troops in Portugal, he had helped England's traditional ally resist a Spanish invasion and performed brilliantly as second in command to Brigadier General John Burgoyne. Thereafter, he had served as a soldier of fortune in the Polish and Russian armies, winning the more or less honorary title of major general. Well educated, Lee spoke French fluently, handled Latin and Greek with ease, and could quote military experts from Xenophon to Frederick the Great.

From the moment he plunged into the dispute between the colonies and the mother country, Lee played an extremist's role. Aside from his temperamental instability, which some biographers think he inherited from an eccentric mother who all but ignored him as a boy, Lee nursed an almost pathological hatred of George III and the men around him, because he had never won the advancement he felt he

13

deserved for his exploits against the French and the Spanish. He called America the "last and only asylum" of liberty, bought land in Virginia near the estate of another ex-British army officer, Horatio Gates, and travelled up and down the eastern seaboard hobnobbing with such American leaders as Samuel Adams in Boston, Alexander McDougall in New York, and Benjamin Rush in Philadelphia. He used his fluent pen to demolish an influential conservative, Dr. Myles Cooper, president of King's College (now Columbia University). In "A Friendly Address to All Reasonable Americans," Cooper had argued that the colonists could not possibly hope to withstand the power of the professionally trained British army. Lee ridiculed this notion with a dazzling combination of mockery and military examples. His pamphlet was widely reprinted and did much to diminish the awe Americans felt for the supposedly invincible British regulars.

When the war finally broke out, Lee was one of the four men considered for the supreme command of the American army. His British birth finally disqualified him, but more than a few delegates to the Continental Congress insisted that the future of the Revolution depended on Lee's becoming Washington's second in command. The prevailing opinion about Washington and Lee at this time can be glimpsed in a letter written by Elbridge Gerry saying that Washington would be acceptable as a commander of the army besieging the British in Boston, but that a "regular" general was also required to give the volunteers the training they so desperately needed.

Lee was undoubtedly the man Congress had in mind for this task. Artemas Ward of Massachusetts was nominated as a sop to New England's pride, but when ill health soon forced Ward to retire, Lee became the senior major general. He served with distinction throughout the siege of Boston, then went south to lead the garrison at Charleston against a British attack in June, 1776.

Later in the summer, with Washington and his army reeling under a series of defeats around New York, Congress ordered Lee to hurry to his support. He played a leading role in persuading Washington to retreat from Manhattan Island and gave good advice at the Battle of White Plains. But the British capture of Fort Washington and its nearly 3,000 men caused Lee to lose almost all faith in Washington's military ability. As the American Commander in Chief retreated through New Jersey, Lee, left in Westchester County with half the army, corresponded with Adjutant General Joseph Reed, who also had nearly given up on Washington. "I do think it is entirely owing to you that this army & the liberties of America so far as they are dependant upon it are not totally cut off,"

Reed wrote. Lee accepted the compliment and agreed that "eternal defeat and miscarriage must attend the man of the best parts if curs'd with indecision."

When Washington summoned Lee to join him in New Jersey a few weeks later, Lee proceeded to act as if he were running a private war. He disobeyed orders repeatedly, even telling one correspondent he was ready to commit "a brave, virtuous kind of treason" to rescue the Revolution. He moved at a snail's pace through New Jersey, attempting to use his small force to revivify local resistance, which had collapsed at the sight of Washington's headlong flight beyond the Delaware. As late as December 8, 1776, he was still in central New Jersey, telling his Commander in Chief, "The Militia in this part of the Province seem sanguine. If they could be assured of an army remaining amongst 'em, I believe they would raise a considerable number." But Washington had no sympathy with Lee's concept of all-out guerrilla war and again ordered him to cross the Delaware and join the main army. Lee lingered four days more, writing to his old comrade Horatio Gates, "...entre nous a certain great man is most damnably deficient." The morning after he expressed this low opinion of Washington, Lee was captured by a British cavalry patrol. For eighteen months he was a prisoner of war, most of the time living in comfort, trading dinners and witty pleasantries with British army friends in New York.

Exposed to such a prolonged view of the immense effort Great Britain was making to subdue the colonies, Lee altered what had been one of his basic beliefs at the beginning of the war—that it would not last more than a few months because "Great Britain cannot stand the contest." At one point, he actually submitted to the British high command a plan for ending the war with a minimum of bloodshed, by transferring operations to the central colonies of Maryland, Virginia, and Pennsylvania. Exchanged in the spring of 1778, he lobbied in Congress on behalf of the British peace commission headed by Lord Carlisle, which offered repeal of most of the laws that had prodded the colonies into rebellion. But the Americans were no longer interested in accommodation, and Lee was told to stick to his soldiering. So he returned to an army that had just endured the agony of Valley Forge. The battles of Brandywine Creek and Germantown had been fought without him. Although neither of these clashes had been an American victory, they had done much to make professional soldiers out of the men who survived them. Months of hard drilling under Baron Friedrich Wilhelm von Steuben had likewise emboldened the American high command into thinking that their soldiers could stand against the best of the British regulars.

Lee resumed his position as ranking major general with a distinctly opposite opinion. He presented to Washington and Congress a well-reasoned plan for a purely guerrilla war. "If the Americans are servilely kept to the European Plan," he wrote, "they will make an Awkward Figure, be laugh'd at as a bad Army by their Enemy, and defeated in every Rencontre which depends on manoeuvres." He insisted that the idea "that a Decisive Action in fair Ground may be risqued is talking Nonsense." Instead, he recommended mov-

Thaddeus Kosciusko, the famous Polish volunteer, gave free vent to his feelings about Lee in this caricature, "The Suspended General."

ing the army west of the Susquehanna and the capital to Pittsburgh if necessary.

These ideas struck Washington and his generals as more than a little quaint. The British, far from preparing to strike a hammer blow at the American army, were in a state of near panic. Thanks largely to the capture of Burgoyne's army at Saratoga, France had entered the war. A French fleet was en route to America, and the new British commander—fat, fussy Sir Henry Clinton—had been ordered to evacuate

Philadelphia and concentrate his army at New York. The question before the American high command was not one of retreat and reorganization, but of whether the revived Continental Army should let Clinton go unmolested or attempt to strike a blow while the British were strung out in a vulnerable line of march.

Washington called a council of war on June 17, the day before Clinton was to evacuate Philadelphia. Lee, partially through his position as senior general and partially through his ability to talk faster, louder, and longer than anyone else, dominated the discussion. His overbearing opinion was probably delivered in the spirit of a letter that he had written shortly before to the president of the Continental Congress: "I am persuaded (considering how he [Washington] is surrounded) that he cannot do without me." Lee emphatically denounced the idea of attacking Clinton. He argued that with the French in the war the Americans had nothing to gain and everything to lose by risking a general engagement. From a purely strategic point of view it was hard to disagree with this reasoning, and in written opinions all the general officers except Anthony Wayne recommended nothing more daring than "a partial stroke" at the retreating British.

But as Clinton lumbered across New Jersey with a supply train some twelve miles long, he was a very tempting target. Washington called another council of war on June 24. Once more Lee vehemently opposed a fight, protesting that instead he would like to build "a bridge of gold" to speed the British across the Hudson to New York. This time there were signs of far more resistance to Lee's ideas among the other general officers. Wayne reiterated his desire to attack. The Marquis de Lafayette urged a blow by a strong detachment on the British baggage train or rear guard. But Lee's obstinacy blunted these more aggressive opinions, and the council broke up agreeing to avoid a general engagement and merely to send 1,500 men "to act as occasion may serve, on the enemy's left flank and rear." Colonel Alexander Hamilton snorted that "the result . . . would have done honor to the most honorable body of midwives and to them only." That night Washington received a private letter from Major General Nathanael Greene, a man whose opinions he respected. "People expect something from us and our strength demands it," Greene wrote. "I am by no means for rash measures but we must preserve our reputations and I think we can make a very serious impression without any great risk and if it should amount to a general action, I think the chance is greatly in our favor."

This was the voice of a new American confidence talking—a voice that Lee lacked the inclination to

CONTINUED ON PAGE 83

COLLECTION OF AND PHOTOGRAPHED BY JAMES R. MEYER

OF MUGS & MEN

"Of a thousand shavers," said Samuel Johnson, "two do not shave so much alike as not to be distinguished." And even today, despite such drearily standardizing influences as the aerosol shaving-cream can and, worse, the electric razor, shaving essentially remains a matter for each man to settle in his own way. But individual expression in tonsorial accouterment was in far fuller flower in the nineteenth and early twentieth centuries, and personal shaving mugs became the rage. They were ordered through one's barber, and oftener than not were kept on a rack at his shop, where one went for his daily shave. Mug decoration went through a number of ever-fancier stages, reaching an apogee with the "occupational" variety, specimens of which are shown above. For five dollars or so, a man could identify himself by trade or profession (Müller the iceman, Field the dentist), by the name of his firm (Spangler & Sons, sawyers), or by avocation (baseball, horse racing, motorcycling). Most designs were hand-painted from bare outlines; the second mug from the right in the top row is rare in that the image of Mr. Kurz, himself a photographer, is reproduced photographically; this type was much favored by politicians and office seekers. Some customers probably got all lathered up just looking at Dr. Goodwin's mug, which bristles with macabre humor.

'Our Little War with the Heathen'

Our *first* Korean war, in 1871, was fought to open the Hermit Kingdom to Western trade. But the hermits wanted very much to be left alone

By ALBERT CASTEL *and* ANDREW C. NAHM

In the chapel of the U.S. Naval Academy at Annapolis there is a plaque:

> In Memory of
> Hugh W. McKee
> Lieutenant U.S.N.
> Born April 23, 1844
> Died June 11, 1871
> from wounds received the same day on the parapet of
> The Citadel, Kanghoa Island, Corea;
> while leading heroically the assault of the
> Naval Battalion
> of the
> U.S. Asiatic Fleet
> erected by his brother officers of the squadron

Most people who read these words are somewhat puzzled: how was it that an American naval officer was killed fighting in Korea in 1871? Not many today are aware that long before 1950 the United States waged a brief but bloody war in that unhappy land.

In the nineteenth century, Korea was often and appropriately referred to as the "Hermit Kingdom." By 1860 it was the last important Asiatic country still closed to the Western powers. In fact its only normal diplomatic and economic contact with the outside world was through China, which exercised an ill-defined suzerainty over it. The only Westerners who had been able to penetrate its confines were a handful of missionaries, who had entered in defiance of Korean laws and were subjected to constant persecution.

The Koreans were determined to preserve their isolation. They knew little of the West, and what they knew they disliked. To them the "shorthairs," as they contemptuously dubbed all Westerners, were mere barbarians whose presence in their land would constitute a source of danger and corruption. Commodore Matthew Calbraith Perry, at the head of a powerful American naval squadron, had journeyed to Japan in 1853 and 1854, returning with a commercial treaty that opened up Japan to the Western world; an active trade between China and the West had been going on for many decades. Japan and even great China might have admitted foreigners, but Korea? Never!

Unfortunately for the Koreans, their desire to be left alone ran counter to the ambitions of Western merchants, missionaries, and ministries, as well as to

Below: These two wounded warriors were among the very few Koreans captured by the Americans. Most of their comrades fought to the death or committed suicide to avoid being taken alive. At left are two marines, Private Purvis and Corporal Brown, who in capturing the Korean flag behind them won the Medal of Honor. With them on the Colorado is an unidentified sailor with the Stars and Stripes.

the realities of international life. It was only a question of time before one or another of the powers attempted to open up the peninsular kingdom. Ironically, it was the Koreans themselves who provided the excuse.

Early in 1866 the reactionary *taewŏngun* (regent to his young son, King Kojong, and the real ruler of the country at the time) instituted a persecution of Christians, during which several French Catholic missionaries were tortured and then beheaded. On learning of these atrocities, the French minister to China sent a naval expedition against Seoul, Korea's royal capital. But when French marines assaulted the forts guarding the river passage to Seoul, they were repulsed,

assert American power in Korea. He first proposed to Paris a joint United States-French intervention, but Napoleon III's government (which understandably enough had no desire to co-operate with the nation that had just forced it out of Mexico) declined the offer. The Secretary then instructed his nephew, George F. Seward, consul general at Shanghai, to journey to Seoul and secure "redress" for the *General Sherman* "outrage." Young Seward, however, reported that such a mission would be futile unless backed by force. Accordingly the Navy, at the State Department's request, ordered a number of ships to the Orient for this purpose.

Seward left office in 1869, before the organization of

with heavy losses. This victory elated the Koreans, increased their contempt for all white-skinned "barbarians," and strengthened their determination to resist foreign "contamination."

Just prior to the French fiasco, an American-owned merchantman, the *General Sherman,* had put into the Taedong River on the northwest coast of Korea. Ostensibly she came to trade, but the Koreans were suspicious that her real object was to rob the graves of their ancient kings. Moreover, the *Sherman*'s crew (mainly Malays and Chinese) probably provoked the local inhabitants. In any case, the natives seized the ship, burned her, and massacred all aboard.

Precise details of the fate of the *General Sherman* and her people did not come to light for many years, but news of her loss, and of the failure of the French expedition, reached Washington late in 1866. Secretary of State William H. Seward, a strong believer in Manifest Destiny, decided that the time had come to

a Korean expedition could be completed, but his successor, Hamilton Fish, went ahead with plans for such an expedition, though he broadened its aims. American merchants in China were urging that the peninsula be opened to trade, and the Russians and Japanese were moving in the same direction. On April 20, 1870, Fish wrote to Frederick F. Low, United States minister to China, instructing him to proceed to Seoul with units of the Asiatic Squadron. His primary goal would be to obtain guarantees of humane treatment for shipwrecked sailors, but he was also to seek a commercial treaty. Fish cautioned him to employ force only if it was necessary to uphold the honor of the flag.

A stout, vigorous New England Yankee, Low was brand-new to his post and totally lacked previous diplomatic experience. But he was a man of substance: at the age of forty-two he had already been a successful banker, a United States congressman, and the Republican governor of California from 1863 to 1867, during which time he had championed the cause of fair treatment for California's Chinese population, rescued Golden Gate Park in San Francisco from land speculators, and played a key role in founding the University of California at Berkeley. Furthermore, in his early youth he had spent five years clerking in a Boston shipping firm employed in the China trade and so perhaps had acquired, secondhand at least, some inkling of Oriental ways. All in all, therefore, he seemed a good choice for the difficult and delicate task of opening up Korea.

The same might have been said of Rear Admiral John Rodgers, commander of the Asiatic Squadron, Low's escort to Korea. A thickset man who wore

ing which Low conferred with Rodgers at Peking and sent word to the king of Korea, via the Chinese, of his intended visit and its purpose. He also collected all available information on that unknown country's "semi-barbarous and hostile people," but as he subsequently wrote to Secretary Fish, "Corea is more of a sealed book than Japan was before Commodore Perry's visit."

Finally, on May 8, 1871, he sailed from Shanghai, accompanied by two Chinese-speaking secretaries, Edward B. Drew and James B. Cowles, Jr. Four days later he boarded Rodgers' flagship, the *Colorado*, in the harbor of Nagasaki, Japan. Riding at anchor alongside the *Colorado* were the other vessels of the Asiatic

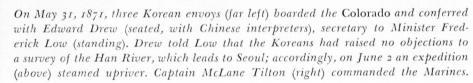

On May 31, 1871, three Korean envoys (far left) boarded the Colorado *and conferred with Edward Drew (seated, with Chinese interpreters), secretary to Minister Frederick Low (standing). Drew told Low that the Koreans had raised no objections to a survey of the Han River, which leads to Seoul; accordingly, on June 2 an expedition (above) steamed upriver. Captain McLane Tilton (right) commanded the Marines.*

a fringe of white whiskers about his stubborn chin, Rodgers at fifty-eight was one of the most experienced and distinguished officers in the Navy. He had served in the Seminole and Mexican wars, conducted the first scientific exploration of the Bering Strait, and during the Civil War had been a skilled and gallant commander of Union ironclad monitors. Nor was he new to the Far East: he had acquired considerable experience there while charting the China Sea and the Sea of Japan in the mid-1850's—experience that included, it is worth noting in view of what was to happen in Korea, the landing of forces on the Liuchiu (Ryukyu) Islands in order to secure the natives' observance of their treaty obligations to the United States. Instructions from Washington gave Low the "responsibility of war or peace" on the forthcoming expedition, but directed him to defer to the Admiral on all naval and military matters.

Planning and preparation took nearly a year, dur-

Squadron: the corvettes *Alaska* and *Benicia* and the gunboats *Monocacy* and *Palos*. Together the five ships mounted eighty-five guns and carried 1,230 sailors and marines. But all were old and obsolescent; the *Colorado*, a steam-and-sail wooden frigate, was in such poor shape that she dared not fire her full broadside for fear of springing her timbers. In addition, only the two gunboats possessed sufficiently shallow drafts to navigate the Han River, the pathway from the sea to Seoul. The three larger ships, therefore, were practically useless except as transports.

Rodgers' force was, as European observers in Nagasaki were quick to point out, far inferior to the one France had sent in 1866, and it was not at all likely to overawe the Koreans. Yet it was about the best the United States could muster in the Far East in 1871. During the Civil War the American Navy was one of the world's most powerful; now, scarcely half a dozen years later, it was in decline, on its way to becoming a national disgrace and an international laughingstock.

Yet if Rodgers' squadron was weak in its ships, it was strong in the quality of its officers and men. They were tough, disciplined, highly trained professionals, most of them veterans of the Civil War. Moreover, from the admiral down to the deckhands they believed that the crews of the *General Sherman* and other vessels had been wantonly murdered; Rodgers' men were determined to compel the Koreans, by force of arms if necessary, to observe the laws of nations and of humanity. They gave little credence to dockside rumors that the Korean soldiers were "ferocious giants" of "herculean strength," and they had no doubts about succeeding where the French had failed. Indeed their

On the morning of May 30 the fleet moved farther up the river and anchored between two islands that the French had named Boisée and Guerrière. "The Country is beautiful," wrote Captain McLane Tilton, commander of the Marine contingent, to his wife, Nannie, back home in Annapolis. "[It is] filled with lovely hills & valleys running in every direction and cultivated with grain of all kinds. . . . Everything is pretty and green, and the little thatched villages are snugly built in little nooks, surrounded by pines & other evergreens."

That afternoon four Koreans approached the *Colorado* in a junk, made signs of friendship, and then came aboard. They brought a document that ac-

Fired upon, the survey party hurried back to the fleet for a council of war with Admiral Rodgers (second from right). When the Koreans refused to apologize, sailors and marines (right) landed, easily took two forts, then had to fight bitterly for a third. Superior American weapons took a heavy toll among the "Tiger Hunters."

mood was in many ways more appropriate to a punitive expedition than to a diplomatic mission.

The little American flotilla steamed out of Nagasaki Bay on May 16 and a week later lowered anchor near the mouth of the Han. Boat parties went ashore and, after demonstrating their peaceful intentions, received a friendly welcome from the natives, who for the first time beheld the "flowery flag" of the "land of Mi." The Americans in turn presented them with gifts of brass buttons, blue cloth, and glass bottles (the last especially prized by the Koreans). They also handed the local prefect a letter stating the purpose of the visit and requesting to see representatives of the King.

Rodgers and Low planned to withdraw from Korea temporarily, after establishing diplomatic contact with the royal court, and then to return for a reply to the American demands. Perry had employed this technique with the Japanese, and they hoped it would prove equally successful with the Koreans.

knowledged receipt of the American letter and announced that the regent was sending some noblemen to hold a conference. The officers of the *Colorado* showed the messengers around the ship, regaled them with food, wine, and ale, and gave them presents. They also persuaded them to pose for photographs, the most interesting of which shows a happily grimacing Korean standing on the deck, arms loaded with empty Bass ale bottles, and clutching a long-stemmed pipe and a copy of *Every Saturday,* a Boston illustrated newspaper with a picture of Senator Charles Sumner of Massachusetts clearly visible on its front page.

The next day three Koreans, ostensibly the pre-announced noblemen, boarded the flagship. They looked important in their wide-brimmed hats and flowing silk robes, and they were carrying small wands, symbols of royal office. But they had no credentials, and questioning revealed that they were of inferior rank. The Koreans were trying the same trick the Japanese had tried on Commodore Perry, and Low reacted in the same way Perry had: he turned the conference over to a secretary, Edward Drew, and retired to his cabin.

Speaking in Chinese, Drew informed the officials that the American minister wished to enter into negotiation with their government, but would treat only with duly accredited persons of equal rank. He further stated—as had Perry in Japan—that on the morrow some survey vessels would ascend the river to take soundings (Rodgers, like Perry, wished to find a safer anchorage). It was hoped, Drew said, that the boats would not be molested.

To this last the officials, Rodgers later recalled,

The steam launches chugged slowly up the river, followed by the *Monocacy* and the *Palos*. The banks on either side were high and densely wooded, with here and there a thatch-roofed village or a rice field. Then, as they approached the lower end of Kanghoa Island, a long line of earthworks and fluttering yellow flags came into view. Soon swarms of white-clad troops could also be seen, as well as scores of straw screens masking batteries of artillery. Through a spyglass an interpreter translated the Chinese characters on the largest of the yellow banners as reading "General Commanding." Evidently the top Korean officer was there in person.

The current at this point in the river was extremely

ALL: NATIONAL ARCHIVES

"made no reply which could indicate dissent"; instead, "their manner of nonobjection conveyed the impression of actual compliance with our wishes." They then bowed politely and took their leave. As a matter of fact they had no authority to say Yes or No to anything. The regent had sent them simply to stall for time, in hopes that the Americans would lose patience and go away. It was the traditional Oriental tactic for dealing with barbarians.

At noon on June 2 the survey expedition set forth. It consisted of the two gunboats, the *Monocacy* and the *Palos*, plus four steam launches armed with howitzers. Although these ships would be passing the main Korean forts guarding the channel to Seoul, Rodgers believed that the envoys' "tacit assurances" of yesterday precluded any danger. Commander Homer C. Blake of the *Palos*, who was in charge of the survey, disagreed. "In ten minutes," he predicted, "we shall have a row."

swift, and it carried the American vessels right past the forts. Suddenly a shot rang out from the parapet flying the "General Commanding" flag. In an instant the screens flew up and some two hundred cannons belched fire and smoke. A storm of lead and iron swept across the river; veterans of the Civil War declared later that it surpassed anything they had ever experienced. Yet only two seamen were wounded and the ships suffered no damage at all. The timing of the barrage had been poor, its aim worse. Moreover, most of the Korean cannons were of small caliber and limited range; mounted in fixed positions, they could not be traversed to hit a moving target.

The Americans promptly returned the fire, the *Monocacy* blasting the forts with eight-inch shells. Under this hammering the Koreans fled in panic, leaving behind numerous dead beside their practically useless guns. Seeing this, Commander Blake at first considered going ahead with the survey as planned,

CONTINUED ON PAGE 72

BRINGING FORTH THE MOUSE

Some Americans may have trouble listing the fifty united states.
Some may be vague about who represents them
in Congress. But it's a sure bet that every one of us—over the age of three—
can identify the nation's most prominent rodent

By RICHARD SCHICKEL

He is called Mickey Sans Culotte in France, Miki Kuchi in Japan, Topolino in Italy, Musse Pigg in Sweden, and Mikel Mus in Greece. He is known to have made an English queen late for tea; to have rescued an American toy-train manufacturer from receivership; to have an emblem, an oath, a handshake, and a song of his own; to be used as a charm to ward off evil spirits among primitive African tribes; and to appear on watches, soap, radiator caps, and innumerable cereal boxes. He is, of course, Mickey Mouse.

His creator, as everyone knows, was Walt Disney, who died on December 15, 1966. Disney made a considerable number of Mickey Mouse cartoon shorts; although immediately popular, they did not make much money in American movie houses. But when Disney shipped his mouse abroad, put him on television, and allowed his cheery countenance to adorn over 5,000 different products, Walt made a fortune.

The actual facts of Disney's life are obscured in the carefully contrived myths released by the zealous publicity department of his studio. In writing the biography from which this article is taken, Richard Schickel notes that he has had "no co-operation from either the Disney family or the Disney organization." The book, to be entitled The Disney Version, *will be published later this month by Simon and Schuster.*

Our article picks up Disney's story in 1927, when the producer was twenty-six years old. After a miserable, dour childhood in Chicago, in Kansas City, and on farms in the Midwest, Walt and his brother Roy (the firm's business manager) came to Hollywood. They set up an animation studio, which they barely managed to keep afloat with two uninspired series: Alice in Cartoonland and later Oswald the Rabbit. The future did not seem promising. —The Editors

There are uncounted versions of the birth of Mickey Mouse, for Walter Elias Disney, and particularly his flacks and hacks, could never resist the temptation to improve upon the basic yarn. This much seems to be true: the idea to use a rodent as the principal character for a cartoon series came to Disney on a train; the year was 1927; and the train was carrying him back to California after a discouraging meeting in New York with Charles Mintz, who was the distributor of both his Oswald and his Alice series. The most flavorsome telling of the tale appeared in an English publication called *The Windsor Magazine* in 1934, under Disney's own by-line, though it is doubtful that he did more than glance at the article his publicity department had prepared for him. The key section began with his boarding the train, with no new contract and no discernible future.

"But was I downhearted?" he inquired. "Not a bit! I was happy at heart. For out of the trouble and confusion stood a mocking, merry little figure. Vague and indefinite at first. But it grew and grew and grew. And finally arrived—a mouse. A romping, rollicking little mouse.

"The idea completely engulfed me. The wheels turned to the tune of it. 'Chug, chug, mouse, chug, chug, mouse' the train seemed to say. The whistle screeched it. 'A m-m-mowaouse,' it wailed. By the time my train had reached the Middle West I had dressed my dream mouse in a pair of red velvet pants with two huge pearl buttons, and composed the first scenario and was all set."

In this 1930's publicity photograph, the multichecked Mr. Disney, his brainchild perched cozily on his biceps, inspects some film. At left is Mickey's girl friend, Minnie. Both first appeared in Plane Crazy, *released in 1929.*

Steamboat Willie, the third Mickey Mouse production, *was the first in which Disney experimented with sound.*

The first Silly Symphony was The Skeleton Dance *(1929). The mice were absent, the music was more sophisticated.*

Camping Out, *made in the early 1930's, introduced two new characters, Clarabelle Cow and Horace Horsecollar.*

It is well known that the name Disney first gave his creation was Mortimer Mouse—borrowed, it is said, from that of a pet mouse he had kept in his Kansas City studio four years before. Disney himself never claimed this, but he frequently confessed "a special feeling" for mice and readily admitted that he had kept a fairly large family of field mice in his Kansas City offices. Originally he had heard their rustlings in his wastepaper basket. He built cages for them, captured them, and allowed one of them who seemed especially bright the occasional freedom of his drawing board. He even undertook a modest training course for the little creature, drawing a circle on a large piece of drawing paper and then tapping the mouse lightly on the nose with a pencil each time he attempted to scamper over the line. Before long Disney had trained him to stay within the circle. When it came time to leave Kansas City, Disney set all of his mice free "in the best neighborhood I could find," as he later put it. Of his parting with his special pet, Disney said that he "walked away feeling like a cur. When I looked back, he was still sitting there, watching me with a sad, disappointed look in his eyes."

There are two versions of the renaming of the cartoon mouse. In the more common one Mrs. Disney reportedly found Mortimer too pretentious and insisted on a less formal-sounding title for the little chap; some say that she suggested the name Mickey, others, that Disney named his new character and she approved it during the course of their long train ride back to California. The other story is far more prosaic; it is simply that one of the first distributors Disney approached liked the idea but not the name, and his objection caused Disney to rename his creation.

In any case, it is certain that immediately after he returned from New York, Disney set his little studio to work on a cartoon that had a mouse as its principal figure. "He had to be simple," Disney later said, discussing the details of the mouse's creation.

We had to push out 700 feet of film every two weeks, so we couldn't have a character who was tough to draw. His head was a circle with an oblong circle for a snout. The ears were also circles so they could be drawn the same, no matter how he turned his head.

His body was like a pear and he had a long tail. His legs were pipestems and we stuck them in big shoes [also circular in appearance] to give him the look of a kid wearing his father's shoes.

We didn't want him to have mouse hands, because he was supposed to be more human. So we gave him gloves. Five fingers looked like too much on such a little figure, so we took one away. That was just one less finger to animate.

To provide a little detail, we gave him the two-button

pants. There was no mouse hair or any other frills that would slow down animation.

In short, the mouse was very much a product of the current conventions of animation, which held that angular figures were well-nigh impossible to animate successfully, and that clearly articulated joints were also too difficult to manage, at least at the speed of drawing that was demanded by the economics of the industry. Hence the strange appearance of many old cartoons when we glimpse them today on television—the thick round bodies contrasting so oddly with the rubbery limbs of the characters. Within a few years, thanks largely to the leadership of the Disney studio, these conventions were abandoned. Whatever economic advantages these early techniques provided were offset, Disney later said, by the fact that they made it "tougher for the cartoonists to give him [Mickey Mouse] character."

Indeed, it is possible that the mouse would have had a life no longer than many of his competitors if a technological revolution had not intervened and presented Disney with an opportunity particularly suited to his gifts and interests. He seized it with an alacrity shown by few in Hollywood. *Plane Crazy,* in which both Mickey and Minnie Mouse made their first appearance, was on the drawing boards on October 6, 1927, when Warner Brothers came out with *The Jazz Singer,* which though not actually the first sound film was the first to integrate sound with story. Only a small part of the dialogue was recorded, but all the musical sequences were, and the result was a sensation. Warner's immediately added similar sequences to three other movies the studio then had in production and laid plans for an all-talking picture. The rest of the industry formally agreed to fight the "Warner Vitaphone Peril," as the innovation was labelled by a trade magazine. The movie makers had been dragging their feet about sound ever since the first practical sound system was invented in 1923, but by the spring of 1928 opposition had collapsed and all the studios were rushing into production with sound pictures. There was nothing dignified or even very intelligent about the transition period. It was, indeed, a hysterical scramble in which Walt Disney and his problems, never in the forefront of anyone's mind, were almost entirely lost from view.

At this point the frugality of Walt and Roy Disney paid off. Between them they had between $25,000 and $30,000 in personal assets, and their studio, though not wildly successful, could afford to go ahead with its first three Mickey Mouse films even though they had no contract for them nor any real idea of who might be persuaded to distribute them. In addition, they were in somewhat the same position as the nearly

After sound and an enlarged cast came color. The Brave Little Tailor (1938) was an early Technicolor attempt.

In Tugboat Mickey, *the mouse played straight man to two newer and funnier characters, Donald Duck and Goofy.*

Fantasia, *in 1940, was Disney's highest-browed effort. As the Sorcerer's Apprentice, Mickey was a natural.*

bankrupt Warner Brothers had been—they had nothing to lose by experimenting with sound: their investment in films not yet released was negligible, they had no investment in actors whose vocal qualities might be unsuitable to the microphone, and the animated cartoon was a medium ideally adaptable to sound. The early sound camera was all but immobile in the soundproof "blimp" that was necessary to prevent its whirrings from being picked up by the microphone. Disney, of course, had no such problem. The animation was shot silently, as always, and sound was added later. This meant that his little films retained their ability to move, unhampered by a stationary camera. Just as important was the control he could exercise over the co-ordination of picture and sound. They could be perfectly integrated by matching the musical rhythm to the rhythm of the drawn characters' movements.

Disney hesitated only briefly before plunging into sound film production. After *Plane Crazy,* he shot a second silent film, *Gallopin' Gaucho,* but in his third, *Steamboat Willie,* he began to experiment with sound.

His chief assistants were Ub Iwerks, in those days getting a "drawn by" credit on the title card of each film, and Wilfred Jackson, a newly employed animator who liked to play the harmonica in his spare time. *Steamboat Willie* was plotted to the tick of a metronome, which set rhythms for both Jackson, who played standard, public-domain tunes on his mouth organ, and for Iwerks, who could plan the animation with the appropriate tempo. The ratio of drawings to bars of music was thus calculated far more simply than it would be only a few years later. To further enliven the sound track, Disney rounded up tin pans, slide whistles, ocarinas, cowbells, nightclub noisemakers, and a washboard. When the animation was finished, the co-workers invited their wives to the studio to see something new one evening, then ducked behind a screen

and played their "score" live, through a sound system Iwerks concocted out of an old microphone and the loudspeaker of a home radio. In later years Disney recalled that the ladies had been vaguely complimentary but had not allowed their husbands' novelty to distract them from girl talk about babies, menus, hairdressers, and so on. Like so many of Disney's reminiscences, this story seems a little too pat to be credible, but, on the other hand, the performance was probably not terribly impressive at that early stage.

By early September, 1928, however, Disney was ready to head for New York again, first in search of someone to put his perfected score on a sound track, and second to find a distributor. By this time Disney and his co-workers had their complete score, down to the last rattle of a cowbell, on paper and had devised a system by which a conductor could keep his beat precisely on the tempo of the film. Sound speed was standardized at ninety feet of film per minute, or twenty-four frames per second. The musical tempo was two beats per second, or one every twelve frames. On the work print that Disney took to New York with him, a slash of India ink was drawn on every twelfth frame, causing a white flash to appear on the screen every half second. All a conductor had to do was to key his beats to the flash; in theory, if he never missed a flash he would reach the end of his strange-looking score at the exact moment the film ended.

To obtain his sound track, Disney first had to find someone willing to record it, and then someone to conduct it—a conductor who would sacrifice the most important variable at his command, tempo, to a gang of musically illiterate cartoonists. Neither was easy to find. The best sound system was controlled by Radio Corporation of America; although it was willing to take Disney's work, it was unwilling to follow his score. Its technicians had already added tracks to some old silent cartoons and were convinced, apparently, that close synchronization between music and sound effects

Behind the scenes dozens—and later hundreds—of people worked to create the cartoons. At left below, Disney presides over a story conference. Next, one artist models faces for a fellow animator. (Could this

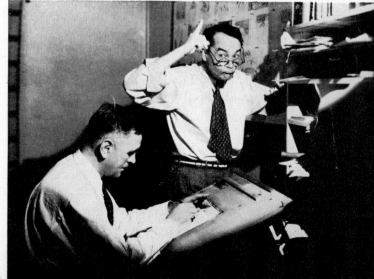

and the action on the screen was, if not impossible, certainly not worth the effort. Disney knew otherwise and refused to relinquish his precious piece of film to them. The R.C.A. men, on the other hand, were not about to let a stranger tell them their business.

Disney then started on the rounds of those entrepreneurs who owned outlaw sound equipment—that is, recording devices either not covered by or not yet restrained by the patents controlled by R.C.A. or its chief rival, Western Electric. Here history was repeating itself, for the first silent cameras and projectors had been controlled by Edison and licensed only to producers and theatres belonging to his so-called "trust." His invention had been so attractive that in spite of Edison's fight to enforce his rights, the trust had been effectively demolished by the sheer number of competitors who violated it. The situation in the sound business never grew quite so unmanageable, for both the quality of the patented systems and the power of the firms that controlled them was such that it was to everyone's advantage to end the in-fighting. But it was impossible to control everyone, and Disney had no real difficulty locating someone to take on his recording chores.

The man he found was a semilegendary figure named Pat Powers, who had learned the movie business—and his code of ethics—in the freebooting days before World War I. It is said, perhaps apocryphally, that Powers, who at one time distributed Carl Laemmle's Universal Pictures, actually resorted to throwing his account books out a twelfth-story window rather than let Laemmle, who got to wondering where his profits had gone, take a look at them. It is also said that Powers had the foresight to have a man waiting in the street below to retrieve the books and make a getaway with them. Disney was to experience some of this buccaneering style during his association with Powers, but he appears to have known what he was getting into, and Powers did have a sound system to put at Disney's service—the "Powers Cinephone."

Powers agreed to let Disney supervise the recording session. He engaged a conductor, Carl Edwardi, the bandleader at the Capitol Theatre; he hired the musicians; and he handled all the details, including the price—$210 per hour for the thirty-member orchestra, plus fees for four sound-effects men and for the technicians. The first session went badly. The bass player's low notes kept blowing tubes, and Disney himself, while doing the Mickey Mouse voice (as he was always to do), blew another when he coughed into an open mike. Worst of all, Edwardi flatly refused to key his beat to the flashes on the screen, no doubt reasoning that a man of his reputation ought to be able to conduct, without the aid of childish prompting devices, a score consisting of "Yankee Doodle," "Dixie," "The Girl I Left Behind Me," "Annie Laurie," and "Auld Lang Syne." After three hours and some $1,200 in costs, they still had nothing usable on the track. Powers, who had promised to pay all excess costs should Edwardi not live up to his reputation, then declared that his offer did not include the musicians' salaries—it was to cover only the cost of the sound equipment and the film. Disney had no choice but to wire his brother for more money. To raise it, Roy Disney sold, among other things, Walt's Moon cabriolet, an automobile with red and green running lights, of which Walt was particularly fond. At the next session Edwardi agreed to try following the flashes on the screen and Disney cut the orchestra almost in half (dispensing with the bothersome string bass, among other instruments) and dismissed two of the sound-effects men, taking over some of their functions himself. This time, everything worked out as planned, and within days Disney was making the rounds of the New York distributors, trying to get someone to handle *Steamboat Willie* for him.

It was a disappointing business. In that year of the great sound crisis a man with a cartoon short subject, even one with an artful sound track on it, did not have

CONTINUED ON PAGE 90

be a Pluto pose?) The serious young woman is checking a sequence of drawings to see that the movement is smooth, while at right below, a musical director conducts a recording session for a sound track.

GRASS

The wheels of westering
settlers moved through an ocean
of grass. It was a rich
natural heritage, but within
a century we almost destroyed it

Text by WILLIAM COTTER MURRAY
Photographs by STEVEN C. WILSON

"As far as the eye could reach, in every direction, there was neither tree, nor shrub, nor house, nor shed visible; so that we were rolling on as it were on the bosom of a new Atlantic, but that the sea was of rich green grass and flowers, instead of the briny and bottomless deep." Thus James Silk Buckingham, a British traveller, described America's Great Plains in 1837. This was the same "Atlantic of grass" that the homesteaders saw, and the longhorns when they spread over the open range up from the South—an ocean of grass to be grazed. There were homesteads to be developed, cattle empires to be expanded, and wheat fields to be plowed deep and combined. The grass grew naturally; it did not need to be cultivated. Who could imagine the broad green ocean drying up?

The Great Plains used to be one of the richest natural grasslands of the world. From the Saskatchewan-Manitoba line it extended south along the ninety-eighth meridian to the Gulf of Mexico and all the way west to the Rockies, taking in eastern Montana, Wyoming, Colorado, and New Mexico, the western part of the Dakotas, Nebraska, Kansas, and Oklahoma, and the Texas Panhandle—"The Great American Desert," it was designated on the maps of the early 1800's. And it was all public domain. We owned the grass and had a rich heritage, but within a century after Buckingham's visit we had almost destroyed it.

The grass kept the Plains in place, kept them from becoming a real desert. It was as simple as that. In an environment with a maximum annual rainfall of only twenty inches and an evaporation rate as high as sixty per cent, there was a hairline balance between sun, water, rivers, soil, wind, and grass. The grass—putting down its roots four, even six feet into the soil, improving its structure, ventilating it, letting water penetrate it, keeping moisture loss low—held the balance of power and kept the environment from destroying itself. During the summer months the rain fell in thunderstorms, hailstorms even; water rushed in torrents down from the Rockies, carried by the Red River, the Platte, the Missouri. Against that force of water nothing could stop the erosion of the soil, nothing but a good thick carpet of grass to hold it down.

Through the ages, nature had laid down such a carpet—native grasses capable of withstanding the special conditions of the environment. They lay dormant through drought and came back above ground when water came again. Some grasses grew in the warm seasons, others in the cool. They could grow with little moisture, hoarding what they got. Over the centuries they had struggled for survival in the Great Plains, adapted to the environment, and thrived.

The environment is diverse. The Great Plains are not all on one level: from an altitude of 5,500 feet up against the Rockies they flatten out going eastward at ten feet per mile. They embrace sand hills, loessal plains, buttes, "badlands," depressions, and rolling flatlands treeless and without protection from the sun except for the grass. The precipitation is uncertain. Temperatures range from 60° below to 120° above. The Plains were formed when the great Cretaceous seas withdrew along the continent and the Rocky Mountains were uplifted, preventing moisture from the Pacific from penetrating eastward. The area gradually dried up; mountain streams cut valleys and ridges through it and grew into rivers that spilled out onto the Plains. There evaporation was so high, rain so scarce, and the land so flat that the rivers lost their force, deposited their burden of mountain soil in aprons over the land, and dribbled on into shallow streams and mudholes or buffalo wallows, where many a settler's wagon got stuck up to its axles.

The grasses that took root and kept the soil from washing away were of several types. In the Northern Plains (roughly Montana, Wyoming, and the western Dakotas) and in the High Plains (the eastern third of Colorado and New Mexico and the western part of Oklahoma) there were the short grasses: buffalo grass, blue grama, three-awns, curly mesquite. Farther east, the longer mid-grasses took root: little bluestem, needle grass, wheat grasses. In the Low Plains—the region's eastern third, along the twenty-inch rainfall line that runs from the eastern Dakotas southward to western Texas—big bluestem and other tall grasses thrived. The plainsman will recognize minor grasses in the kingdom with colorful names like bottlebrush, red ray, fool hay, pancake, jungle rice, panic grass. The environment created these grasses; they are natives—the original natives, which were there even before the buffalo and the Indian came.

Coronado saw the grasses in 1541 in his abortive search for gold in the Seven Cities of Cibola. He and his army almost got lost among them; as soon as they passed, the grasses straightened. Men who wandered away from the army train got lost. Finally Coronado gave up on the Plains; there was no gold there, and it was too cold. The grass was good for the expedition's cows, but there was no civilization there to conquer.

The Indians inhabited the Plains before Coronado came and remained after he passed. Thirty-one tribes held sway there, each somehow able to read the landscape so that they recognized one another's territories. We can order the succession of invaders of the Great Plains like this: first, the soil came from the Rockies, then the grasses grew, then the buffalo came down from the north for the grasses, then the Indians fol-

TEXT CONTINUED ON PAGE 81

32

THE DECLINE AND RISE OF THE GRASSLANDS

The Great Plains, embracing all or parts of ten states and constituting over one-tenth of the total land area of the United States, were once covered with lush grasses sprung from soil carried by rivers *(above)* that began with a rush high in the Rocky Mountains and ended in broad meanderings across the horizonless flatlands. In less than a hundred years of occupation by the white man, the delicate balance between the grasses and their environment was badly upset. The story of that near-disaster and of the hopeful restoration now well begun is told on the next fourteen pages. The photographs are by Steven C. Wilson; the words, for the most part, are those of men and women who down through the years have known and loved the Plains. —*The Editors*

LAND, INDIAN, BUFFA

"It is almost impossible for a civilized being to realize the value to the Plains Indian of the Buffalo," wrote Colonel Richard Irving Dodge in 1882. "It furnished him with home, food, clothing, bedding, horse equipment, almost everything." The great beasts once covered the Plains, but despite their num-

34

NATURAL BALANCE

bers they did not overgraze it. Dodge noted that "when the food in one locality fails, they go to another, and towards fall, when the grass of the high prairie becomes parched up by heat and drought, they gradually work their way back to the South . . . whence . . . they are ready to start . . . northward [again]."

THE DAY OF THE LONGHORN

"This ain't no country fer little two-by-four farmers," an old-time Texas cattleman said. ". . . The big thing about the plains is that you don't have to feed stock. It can rustle fer itself. You can yoke it up with stepmaw Nature an' the pair, if they wants to, can make the dollars crawl into yer jeans." The grazing lands, it seemed, were inexhaustible. And so, after the Civil War, the great herds of longhorns started up the long trail from Texas to the Kansas railheads, cropping the grass as they went. But within twenty years, trouble was apparent. In 1886, in one of his serious moments, the western humorist and journalist Bill Nye wrote: "Let me warn the amateur cowman that in the great grazing regions it takes a great many acres of thin grass to maintain the adult steer in affluence for twelve months, and the great pastures at the bases of the mountains are pretty well tested. Moreover, I believe that . . . cattlemen . . . will tend to overstock the ranges at last, and founder the goose that lays the golden egg." His prediction turned out to be true: overgrazing—coupled with an unusually severe winter the following year—ended the palmy days of the cattle business.

THE PLOW AND THE FENCE

Meanwhile the "little two-by-four farmers," encouraged by the Homestead Act of 1862 and its later liberalizations, were crowding into the Great Plains, plowing up the grass and fencing in the pasturelands. "Now there is so much land taken up and fenced in that the trail for most of the way is little better than a crooked lane," a trail driver lamented, "and we have hard lines to find enough range to feed on. These fellows from Ohio, Indiana, and other northern and western states—the 'bone and sinew of the country,' as politicians call them—have made farms, enclosed pastures, and fenced in water holes until you can't rest; and I say, D—n such bone and sinew! They are the ruin of the country, and have everlastingly, eternally, now and forever, destroyed the best grazing-land in the world." Grasslands that should never have been plowed dried up when cycles of drought rolled around; in 1874, to add to the farmer's woes, came a plague of grasshoppers ("Thirty acres of wheat which looked beautiful and green in the morning is eaten up," said a Kansas homesteader sorrowfully). The final reckoning was delayed, but eventually it would come.

In the early 1930's, unusually severe droughts occurred, followed by dust storms such as the Plains had never experienced. "Little by little," wrote John Steinbeck in *The Grapes of Wrath,* "the sky was darkened by the mixing dust, and the wind felt over the earth, loosened the dust, and carried it away. . . . The dawn came, but no day." When at length the day did come, its light revealed a terrible desolation *(overleaf)* that is still visible in parts of the Plains.

THE GOVERNMENT TAKES A HAND

"The problem of the Great Plains," wrote President Franklin D. Roosevelt in 1937, "is not merely one of relief of a courageous and energetic people who have been stricken by several years of drought during a period of economic depression. . . . The problem is one of arresting the decline of an agricultural economy not adapted to the climatic conditions because of lack of information and understanding at the time of settlement and of readjusting that economy in the light of later experience and of scientific information now available." Together ranchers, farmers, and Department of Agriculture experts took stock of the desolation. They set up federal grass nurseries and developed new methods of reseeding. Nature helped. "This year, once more," wrote Stanley Vestal in 1941, "the hopefulness and confidence of the people of the High Plains is justified. The drouth is over, the rains are falling, turning the Dust-Bowl gold and green again. A thousand pulpits resound with the words of the prophet Joel: 'Fear not, O land; be glad and rejoice: for the Lord will do great things.'" With aid from Washington and the Plains people themselves, He has.

THE LAND SMILES AGAIN

After the droughts and dust storms of the 1930's, nearly half the cropland in the Great Plains was badly eroded, and seventy-five per cent of the range was in decline. Three quarters of this desolation is now under active repair, and the good work goes on. The results, throughout the Plains, recall the lines Walt Whitman wrote many years ago: "A child said *What is the grass?* fetching it to me with full hands; / How could I answer the child? I do not know what it is any more than he. / I guess it must be the flag of my disposition, out of hopeful green stuff woven. . . .

…Or I guess it is the handkerchief of the Lord,
A scented gift and remembrancer designedly dropt.''

BUTLER *the* BEAST?

LEAP YEAR AGAIN!

BELLE BUTLER (*a giddy thing*)—"Be still, my poor fluttering little heart! I must Pop the Question again—This is my last chance!"

For nearly fifty years, in one way or another, Ben Butler courted the favor of his state and the nation. He may not have been a bona fide Beauty, but there were times when his traditional nickname did not seem quite fair either

By FRANCIS RUSSELL

The grassy slopes in front of Boston's State House boast no monument to Ben Butler, former governor and Civil War general, though another native son and conspicuously unsuccessful general, "Fighting Joe" Hooker, bestrides his horse in front of the east wing. Butler was not given equal statuary space because, it was felt, he was too well remembered in the flesh—and as a thorn in the flesh—to warrant a reminder in bronze.

Massachusetts memories are long: when James M. Curley stormed his way to the governor's chair in 1934, fifty-two years after Butler, and proceeded to turn the State House and the state upside down, exasperated Republicans proclaimed him "the worst Massachusetts governor since Ben Butler."

The comparison was as apt as it was bitter. Like Curley, Butler was a tribune of the people, assailing and enraging the Beacon Hill plutocracy. Both traded on their Irish ancestry (which in Butler's case had to be invented), and both seemed to leave behind an odor of corruption. Like Curley, Butler had an acute intelligence unfettered by any awkward ethical sense. Both made political hay by championing the underdog. On Governors Butler and Curley, Harvard refused to bestow its customary degree. Legends clustered around each: for

Ben Butler the most persistent—it is still believed in the South—is that when he was recalled as military governor of New Orleans during the Civil War he took with him a coffin filled with stolen silver spoons.

Nothing Curley ever did, however, made him as lastingly notorious as New Orleans General Order No. 28 made Butler. It said, "when any female shall, by word, gesture, or movement, insult or show contempt for any officer or soldier of the United States, she shall be regarded and held liable as a woman of the town plying her avocation."

Butler was military governor of a conquered city, and the provocation had in fact been gross. Northern soldiers were repeatedly insulted by New Orleans women; some of the city's belles had taken to spitting on their uniforms, or even in their faces. But Butler's "Woman Order," while it put a stop to such incidents, made him the most hated of Yankee generals.

The Confederacy's General P. G. T. Beauregard coined the phrase "Butler the Beast," and it stuck. Jefferson Davis, once Butler's friend, proclaimed him "an outlaw and common enemy of mankind," to be hanged on capture. Long after the war, Mississippi riverboats supplied their cabin passengers with chamber pots on the inside bottoms of which was painted the face of "Spoons Butler."

Benjamin Franklin Butler was a sixth-generation New Englander, born in 1818 in Deerfield Parade, New Hampshire. The youngest of three children by his father's second wife, Ben was a sickly child. He had reddish hair and a pasty face marred by a crossed left eye with a drooping lid, which would give him the unkind sobriquet Old Cock-Eye. He was only five months old when his father died; his mother worked days as a hired woman. She was a devout Baptist, who knew her boy was intelligent and hoped he might become a preacher. For all his gnomish ugliness, Ben had a quick mind and a memory like a mag-

Ben Butler was an enduring target for lampooning cartoonists, as the drawings on these and the following pages indicate. At the left, an 1888 issue of Puck *neatly satirized Butler's ever-ardent aspirations to the Presidency. Four years earlier,* Puck *had depicted him as a clown (right) trailing a sausage-string of nominations so varied as to imply that Butler was willing to affiliate himself with whatever cause or party seemed most expedient at any given moment.*

49

net. Before he entered school he had read *Robinson Crusoe* with his mother's help and could recite whole chapters from the Bible.

When Ben was nine a neighbor persuaded the head of Phillips Exeter Academy to give the boy a scholarship, but Ben's brief stay there was an unhappy, awkward time. He was not, a fellow student remembered, "particularly civil when his grain was crossed." After one term he left for Lowell, Massachusetts, the mill town where his mother now worked as a housekeeper in one of the factory workers' dormitories. Lowell was his home for the next sixty-five years.

Lowell was a model textile settlement, with central factories, company stores, and a company burial lot, as well as employees' dormitories. The city was named after Francis Cabot Lowell, who on a sojourn in England had managed to filch the secrets of British power-loom construction. Although Lowell was their creation, the corporation owners never lived there, but filaments of gold ran from the mills to Boston pockets.

Compared with the "dark Satanic mills" of England's industrial cities, the large-windowed brick factories of Lowell were pleasant places. Most of the mill hands were New England country girls who earned from six to eight dollars a week, sufficient to sustain a single girl and to allow her to do her share in reducing the mortgage on the family farm (see "The Working Ladies of Lowell" in the February, 1961, AMERICAN HERITAGE). Whittier, who lived for a time in Lowell, called these buxom lasses "the flowers gathered from a thousand hillsides and green valleys of New England, fair unveiled Nuns of Industry."

Ben and his older brother, Andrew Jackson Butler, passed their adolescence in the vestal atmosphere of their mother's boardinghouse, attending the Lowell public school, whose master, Joshua Merrill, carried a leather strap to administer the Yankee blend of "licking and learning." Despite his crossed eye, Ben grew solid and tough, handy with his fists and impudent to authority. "Benj. F. Butler was a boy who might be led, but could never be driven," wrote his high school principal. In those early years Ben developed two enduring hatreds: of England, the country against which his grandfather had fought at Bunker Hill; and of the absentee plutocrats of Beacon Hill, the inheritors of British decorum who owned the mills of Lowell and the other spindle cities.

It was arranged for Ben to go to the Baptist college at Waterville, Maine, where he could fulfill his mother's dream of seeing him a preacher. But as a collegian his religiosity ebbed; he took keen interest in philosophy, history, and chemistry, and developed sufficient aptitude for debate to become head of the Literary Society. In Whig New England he proclaimed himself a Jacksonian Democrat, scornful nevertheless of the abolitionists and their incendiary agitation. Politics intrigued him, and his interest in the law was aroused when he attended a murder trial and watched the deft maneuverings of the lawyers before the jury. At the end of his sophomore year he applied for an appointment to the United States Military Academy; his rejection left him with a lasting bias against West Pointers. He graduated from Waterville (later Colby) College in 1838 and that fall returned to Lowell eager to become a lawyer.

He began to read law, in the self-educating legal political pattern of Clay and Webster and Lincoln, in the office of William Smith; in exchange for doing clerical chores he was given access to Blackstone and Kent.

For two years he spent over twelve hours a day on his law books. Whenever he grew too restless in his confinement he would borrow a horse and gallop over country roads reciting snatches of Byron, Moore, or Scott to the evening sky. Since the small fees that he picked up handling Smith's debt-collection cases were not enough to live on, he taught school for a term in 1839. Like schoolmaster Merrill, he believed in the strap. While teaching, he became friends with Fisher Ames Hildreth, the son of a local doctor and well-known patriotic orator. Hildreth took Ben home for Thanksgiving dinner.

Dr. Hildreth was a widower with five daughters; the eldest, Sarah, acted as his hostess. She was three years older than Ben, more graceful than handsome, yet witty, animated, and self-possessed. She fascinated him, and within days the two were keeping steady company. At first it went no further than that; Sarah, though promised an adequate dowry, had no intention of marrying until Ben's as yet nonexistent law practice could support

them. She would not say yes to him, although she would not say no, either.

In 1840 Butler took his bar examination, using the occasion to differ with a decision the examining judge had made earlier that very day. Nevertheless, he was admitted to the bar the following day, and to cap it, the judge reversed his finding. The road lay open: Butler was ready to turn Blackstone into gold. He set up his own office in Lowell, where he was soon working eighteen hours a day. Factory girls, ignored by other attorneys, came to him with their petty cases and two- or three-dollar fees. From the first, he disrupted the still-colonial decorum of Massachusetts legal circles; he once spent a week in the Lowell jail after a judge had found him in contempt. Daring, astute, methodical, and unscrupulous, Butler, with his grotesque, rufous exterior, was unforgettable. His manner of speech and easily summoned tears were convincing to juries. The plea of insanity in murder trials was his innovation. He became noted for finding flaws in indictments; he once managed to free a burglar by claiming that a key the man had stolen was not personal property but real estate. When a reporter for the Whig Lowell *Courier* denounced Butler's courtroom tactics as "very scaly and disreputable," Butler stormed into the newspaper office and pulled the reporter's nose.

Butler inspected the letter of the law with his good eye, its spirit with his bad one. When the Lowell City Council passed an ordinance that all dogs must be muzzled, Butler walked his dog with a muzzle attached to its tail. He knew how to court popular favor by belittling Harvard's aristocratic pretensions. Once when asked in court to be more respectful because the witness was a Harvard professor, he told the judge, "I am well aware of that. We hung one of them the other day."

Soon it was being said that the cross-eyed young attorney with the rasping, staccato voice was the man to win hard cases. Special reporters were assigned to cover his sensational courtroom conduct. "He liked audacious surprises," said one of his enemies. "He was seldom content to try a simple case in a simple way." Clients flocked to him. To the mill owners he said, "If I am not for you, I shall be against you; and you can take your choice." Their choice was to hire him, even though he and they remained enemies. By the end of a decade of practice, Butler had become the most spectacular criminal lawyer in New England.

Ben and Sarah were finally married in 1844, and it turned out to be a serene and happy partnership. They had four children, three sons and a daughter (the first-born, Paul, died before he was five). As Butler prospered, he invested in land, mills, and other ventures. When Lowell's first woolen mill, the Middlesex Corporation, found itself in straits, he bought the controlling interest. With the mill came Belvidere, a graceful mansion in the Regency style. Situated in the select hill section above the city, Belvidere overlooked the Merrimack River; from its cupola one could gaze north to the hills of New Hampshire. Butler installed central steam heat—then an astonishing novelty—and a "Russian bath" in his bedroom. Though a lawyer of the people, he led the private life of a country squire.

As Lowell grew, its aspect and character changed. The Nuns of Industry were being replaced by the shanty

As the drawing at far left suggests, the crowning achievement of Butler's one term as governor of Massachusetts was his exposure of abuses at the Tewksbury almshouse (he charged that paupers' corpses were being sold to the Harvard Medical School). The next caricature, from a cartoon called "The Presidential Recruiting Office," has Butler straining to measure up; alas, he can reach only to Notoriety. Butler's Civil War record had not inspired universal admiration, and cartoonists often dressed him in ridiculous uniforms. In the next sketch he poses as the workingman's friend.

51

Irish, the pallid and beaten refugees of the Famine. Faced with an abundance of labor, the operators cut wages. The neat boardinghouses disintegrated into slums, whole families inhabiting rooms where single girls had once lived, while other poor Paddies lived in mud-walled shacks along a common known as the Acre.

Partly out of genuine sympathy and partly from a shrewd realization of their political potential, Butler became the champion of the Lowell workers. He denounced wage reductions, comparing Lowell to a bee-hive from which the Boston proprietors extracted honey without caring "whether the bees were smoked out or not." He advocated a ten-hour day in the interest of the workers' health. The Whig legislature was as unmoved as the mill owners, who insisted that the fourteen-hour day was competitive, and that in any case their job was "to give people as cheap calico as can be made."

In 1844 Butler was a delegate to the Democratic National Convention in Baltimore that nominated James K. Polk. On his return to Lowell he made his first political speech, against Henry Clay, the Whig candidate. His influence as a Hunker Democrat* grew. By 1850 he was one of the state leaders instrumental in forming a coalition with the Free-Soil party. Campaigning for the ten-hour day, the secret ballot, and the popular election of judges, the coalitionists swept the state and elected Democrat George Boutwell governor. By agreement, the Democratic representatives then voted with the Free-Soilers in the legislature to elect the Radical Republican Charles Sumner to the United States Senate. The coalitionists managed to pass a secret ballot law, but Whig maneuvering delayed action on the ten-hour day.

In 1852, another presidential election year, Butler was a Democratic nominee for state representative. In a special run-off election he won a seat, and arrived on Beacon Hill in January, 1853. With the Whigs back in the majority position, however, he was unable to effect much legislation. A ten-hour-day bill died in committee, but Butler scored an indirect victory when the corporations, faced with the growing weight of public opinion against them, voluntarily reduced the mill day to eleven hours.

The fifties found Butler an emergent Democrat on the national scene, a wealthy lawyer with the largest criminal practice in New England, the head of a corporation owning three mills, the owner of the finest house in Lowell, and a full colonel in the volunteer militia. He was not yet forty years old.

In 1855 the "Know-Nothing" governor, Henry J. Gardner, who had been elected on an antiforeigner, anti-Catholic platform, disbanded Butler's Irish militia com-

*They were called Hunkers because they were said to be "hunkering" after jobs. The Hunkers, drawing their support from mill workers (who wanted no competition from freed Negroes), had little use for the abolitionists.

pany and removed Butler from his colonelcy. Surprisingly, the cashiered colonel did not fight back. Secretly, however, he campaigned among his militia comrades, and soon Gardner, much to his chagrin, was forced to sign the commission of the newly elected Brigadier General Butler, commander of the 3rd Brigade, 2nd Division, of the state volunteers. Two years later Secretary of War Jefferson Davis appointed "the youngest general in the United States" to the Board of Visitors of the United States Military Academy. Martial in sword and general's sash—if not in features—Butler appeared annually at West Point with the predictable pride of a civilian in uniform.

Butler was the only Democrat elected to the state senate in 1859. There he reorganized the state judiciary, but most of his time was taken up with local and ephemeral matters, with indirect digs at Harvard, and with measures to please the foreigners who formed the core of his support.

The following year he accepted the Democratic nomination for governor, the first of his seven campaigns for that office. But men who, like Butler, sought to straddle the slavery question had become increasingly repugnant to New England opinion that was more and more solidly abolitionist. Butler received only a third of the 108,000 votes cast.

In the summer of 1860 Butler was a delegate to the Democratic National Convention in Charleston, South Carolina. At that stalemated assembly he voted with his delegation seven times for Stephen Douglas and then gave his solitary vote fifty-seven times to Jefferson Davis, a friend whom he considered a moderate compromise between the intractable Southerners and the smoke-breathing abolitionists.

Massachusetts felt otherwise about the slave-owning Davis, and Butler was hanged in effigy on Lowell's South Common. His attempts at defending himself at a public meeting were booed and hissed. A rump Democratic convention at Baltimore had finally nominated Douglas, the Southern delegates having walked out to nominate Kentucky's John C. Breckinridge. When the anti-Douglas Democrats of Massachusetts nominated Butler for governor on a "Breckinridge" ticket, he received only 6,000 of the 169,534 votes cast. It looked as though Butler were on the wrong ship, and a sinking ship, at that. He held intimate talks with Davis and other Southern leaders; long before most Northern politicians, he realized that secession and war were inevitable. Privately he urged Governor John Andrew to prepare the state militia for war, pointing out, among other things, that the volunteers lacked winter overcoats. Coats were ordered, and by curious coincidence, Butler's were the only mills able to produce the cloth immediately.

Three days after Fort Sumter was fired upon, Secretary of War Simon Cameron, alarmed at Washington's isolation, begged Governor Andrew to send him 1,500 militiamen for the capital's defense. Butler realized that if the men were dispatched in a unit, in a brigade instead of three regiments, they would need a brigadier general to command them. Butler wired Cameron, "You have called for a brigade of Massachusetts troops; why not call for a brigadier general and staff?" Butler also knew that the state treasury lacked the money to mobilize and transport the troops; he influenced a number of Boston banks to advance the funds—on condition that he lead the brigade. Andrew had no option but to place the Lowell lawyer in command. President Lincoln was not displeased to see so prominent a Hunker Democrat in a general's uniform rallying to support the Union, and Butler, in sash and gilt epaulettes, recalled that Presidencies were often won on the battlefield.

Washington lay like a beleaguered island in a Southern sea, and Massachusetts was the first to respond to Lincoln's appeal for troops. Butler dispatched his 6th Regiment ahead as an advance guard. In Philadelphia, Butler learned that the 6th had been attacked as it crossed through Baltimore en route to Washington. Three militiamen had been killed, and eight wounded. The mob had seized control of the city. No more troops could pass through.

Butler acted with vigor and dispatch. He sent the rest of his brigade to Annapolis by sea; he converted the Naval Academy into his base while readying himself to commandeer the railroad line to the capital. The governor of Maryland called a special session of the legislature, and Butler announced that if the members passed an ordinance of secession he would arrest every last man of them. He sent a squad of soldiers to impound the state's Great Seal, without which no legislative act would be legal. With Butler's firm measures and his opening of the railroad to Washington, secessionist sentiment in Maryland abated. In circumventing disloyal Baltimore and in providing Washington with troops, Butler was the first Northern general to make his mark.

Even New England Whigs thought him a hero, and he seemed even more heroic when, on May 13, 1861, he and the Massachusetts 6th seized Baltimore without a casualty. But in so doing Butler had disregarded the operations plan of Winfield Scott, the crusty, ancient General in Chief; Scott demoted Butler to the command of Fortress Monroe, a squat bastion on the Yorktown Peninsula. But to salve the sting, Secretary of War Cameron promoted Butler to major general.

Now Butler had twelve regiments in his command. As an organizer he was efficient and ingenious, and he was determined to make his fortress a model garrison. One of his problems was how to deal with slaves who had escaped to his lines. The property of those in rebellion could be taken as contraband of war; Butler declared that slaves were property, hence "contrabands" and sub-

CONTINUED ON PAGE 75

Bible-oriented drawings of Butler, like these showing him as an avenging angel, as a prophet, and as Moses, were doubly ironic because of his physical grotesqueness. Some Boston Brahmin parents got results by telling their children that Ben Butler—with his toadlike shape and drooping eye—would get them if they didn't behave.

ALL: CULVER PICTURES

53

Among the Clouds

There is a kind of astonishing improbability about the Mount Washington Cog Railway. This New Hampshire institution is so obviously a child of the nineteenth-century world of great white summer hotels with endless porches filled by genteel rockers, that its mere survival in an age of television, expressways, and air-conditioned motels seems almost wondrous. In an age that regards 1,200-mile-an-hour supersonic aircraft as much-needed improvements upon 700-mile-an-hour jets, a transportation system that moves passengers at four miles an hour, with locomotives built in the nineteenth century, borders on fantasy. In an era that has seen family-owned businesses replaced with "multi-management corporate bodies," to quote a recent publicity release, there is something rather quaint about a cog railway that has thrived for ninety-nine years thanks in large part to the efforts of just four men.

Sylvester Marsh, first of the four, the New Hampshireman who planned the railway, said in later years that he undertook the venture to cure his boredom and dyspepsia. The cure has left no mark in the annals of medicine, but it has left a lasting mark upon the mountains of the world, from the Rockies to the Alps. It was the world's first, and is still the world's steepest, cog railway; it is still powered entirely by steam and is still ridden by passengers in the thousands from July to October. Today, as ninety-nine years ago, travellers board the cog railway's one-car trains at the Base Station and are steam-propelled up grades as steep as 37.5 per cent—a rise of 37.5 feet vertically for every 100 feet forward—to the 6,288-foot summit of Mount Washington.

Sylvester Marsh was attacked by boredom and dyspepsia because he acted upon his expressed opinion that when a man has enough money he ought to stop working. In his case, this reasonable pause came in his fifty-second year. Born in 1803 in Campton, New Hampshire, he grew up on a farm, moved (on foot) to Boston before he was twenty, rose to eminence and wealth as a meat packer in the primordial Chicago of 1833, lost his money in the panic of the 1830's, recouped his fortune in grain, and retired to the green Boston suburb of Jamaica Plain.

In August of 1857, he climbed Mount Washington in company with a clergyman friend. A fierce storm broke, and the two men stumbled, exhausted, to shelter at the summit. Such storms are not unusual on Mount Washington; unwary climbers have died of exposure there in August. Yet even at the time of Marsh's ascent, trips to the summit on foot or horseback were popular. It is not unlikely, then, that the nearly disastrous outing set Marsh to pondering the virtues of an easier way to the top. Adding to his interest was a model cogwheel locomotive and cograil-centered track constructed by an acquaintance, Herrick Aiken of Franklin, New Hampshire. Aiken was a fertile and successful inventor; he had already devised a circular knitting machine that produced a seamless stocking in less than five minutes. Aiken had shown his cogwheel locomotive model to working railroaders; then as now a conservative breed, they had dismissed the concept as impracticable.

Marsh, no railroader himself but a practical man—his success in meat packing came after he had invented the necessary machinery—was very impressed with Aiken's model. He promptly had another constructed to his order, a clockwork-powered cogwheel locomotive and eight feet of track, wound it up for a New Hampshire legislative committee, and blandly requested a charter for a railway up Mount Washington. After running the gantlet of heavy-handed legislative jests suggesting that it be extended to permit service to the moon, Marsh's charter was signed on June 25, 1858, by Governor William Haile. The times were not propitious for

Among the Clouds *was the name of a daily summer newspaper edited and printed at the top of Mount Washington for many years starting in 1877. Right: a typical nineteenth-century excursion party steams laboriously up one of the steep stretches.*

54

Tourists who ride the famous cog railway up the precipitous slopes of Mount Washington often feel the sky itself is their destination. Overcoming many obstacles—including a recent serious accident —the little locomotives with their tilted boilers have been huffing and puffing people to New England's highest summit for nearly a century

By JOHN H. ACKERMAN

Sylvester Marsh, who conceived the railway

Walter Aiken, who actually launched it

attracting investors to a bizarre mountain railway. Marsh devoted himself to a research-and-development program. The Aiken model had demonstrated clearly that it was quite feasible to build an engine that could climb a mountain. How to build one that could descend safely was less clear. Marsh's eventual solution was such a triumph of simplicity that it is still in use today. The locomotives become rolling air compressors on the descent. Special valves admit air to the four cylinders of the locomotive; compressed by the pistons, the air holds engine speeds to a safe four miles an hour on the downgrade. Marsh also perfected the locomotives' running gear; it too is still in use today, slightly modified, on all six of the railway's engines.

After the Civil War, a new $500 working model of the cog engine and track—and the belated perception of New England railroads that a cog railway could generate vacation passenger traffic—smoothed Marsh's way, although he had to contribute $5,000 toward the venture himself. Surveys had already indicated that a great ridge on the mountain's flank jutting toward the valley of the Ammonoosuc River would be an ideal path for a railway. Yet building the line proved difficult. From the nearest railroad, twenty-five miles away at Littleton, New Hampshire, men and oxen struggled through the woods with materials, equipment, and supplies. A log

house went up to accommodate the workers. Plans called for the track to be mounted on longitudinal stringers set on crossties, much of it airborne on trestles. There was no sawmill available at first, and ties, stringers, and trestle timbers had to be shaped laboriously by hand. While the track inched up the grade, the first locomotive arrived. Built by Campbell, Whittier & Co. of Boston and based on Marsh's working model, the little engine looked hardly bigger than a model itself. It arrived at the site—formally called Marshfield but more commonly known then and now as the Base Station—in pieces. It had been taken apart for the slow haul through the woods and had to be reassembled. Marsh drove his crews hard during that summer of 1866. By August 29, a quarter-mile of track had been completed, crossing the Ammonoosuc River on a trestle with a grade of 1,700 feet to the mile. It was not much of a stretch for those days of transcontinental railroad building, but it was long enough to justify a trial run in the hope of garnering useful publicity. A flatcar large enough to carry forty people was hastily knocked together, and the diminutive engine, optimistically named *Hero*, was fired up for the run. Because her vertical boiler resembled a pepper-sauce bottle, a bystander promptly nicknamed the engine *Peppersass*.

The brief run was a huge success; the glowing reports

Nobody ever zipped home in greater style after working on the railroad than Mount Washington's crewmen, whose slideboards at times reached fifty miles an hour (left). Below, old Peppersass, *the first engine, pushes materials and a construction crew up an unfinished trestle in 1868. The two views of the Base Station at right show successive ways of arriving at the cog railway's lower terminal from Fabyan, New Hampshire: at first by stagecoach, later by train.*

and further offended the Boston & Maine by its winter hibernation and laborious spring revival. The relationship became especially strained during the Depression. For railroads, it was a particularly disastrous period, since in addition to the over-all business decline they suffered increasing and largely irreplaceable losses of freight and passenger business to autos, trucks, and buses. By 1931, the Boston & Maine had abandoned its branch from Fabyan to the Base Station, and decided to dispose of the cog railway itself.

An offer was first made to sell the line to owners of neighboring hotels. They declined, but one of them, Colonel William A. Barron of Crawford House, suggested the course that ultimately saved the railway. "What you need," he said to a Boston & Maine executive, "is a circus promoter; a man who can run the road, increase services, stir up new business, publicize the railway to get more people interested in taking the trip up Mount Washington." The Boston & Maine found a man so eminently suited for the task that the survival of the cog railway without him cannot be imagined.

At first glance, Colonel Henry N. Teague seemed a somewhat unlikely candidate for the ownership and presidency of an unprofitable part-time railway. He had dropped $1,000,000 in Florida land speculations in the 1920's and, conceivably, would have had difficulty finding the price of a round trip on the cog railway. A native of Maine, he was a graduate of Dartmouth College and one of the first graduates of its Amos Tuck School of Administration and Finance. His colonelcy was honorary; he'd been a private in the Spanish-American War.

Pressed to buy the cog railway, Colonel Teague not surprisingly pleaded poverty. The Boston & Maine then airily presented him with the cog railway and a mortgage for $100,000. When the Colonel pointed out that he lacked cash to operate the line, the Boston & Maine put $10,000 in the bank for him. In return for an IOU of epic proportions in the midst of the worst depression in American history, Henry N. Teague had acquired an unprofitable mountain railway with train sheds full of more or less viable antiques.

Apparently cut out to be a genial bear of a man, the Colonel became less genial and his temper shorter. But he coped admirably. The railway had been running two trains a day to the summit, a schedule geared to the twice-a-day arrival of the branch-line trains from Fabyan, when those were still running. Aware of the greater freedom afforded by private autos, the Colonel began running one train an hour—a schedule that remains substantially unchanged today. To lure passengers, he inundated roadside restaurants, tourist cabins, gasoline stations, and diners with advertising folders. He drove to every convention within reach to promote the line. When he wasn't away promoting, he often sat at the Base Sta-

tion, surveying his domain; when an acquaintance said, "How are you?" the Colonel replied, "Cross as ever."

His crossness was suspect, however. He was genuinely fond of the college boys he recruited annually to run the railway and paid them bonuses at the end of the season. A lonely man who never married, he made the railway and its workers a substitute for a family, and the boys repaid him with loyalty and affection. His skills at promotion soon doubled the annual passenger traffic. He enlarged the parking lot at the Base Station and built comfortable cabins, a restaurant, and a gift shop.

Henry Teague proved the wisdom of the Boston & Maine in choosing him to shoulder a burden it could no longer bear. But he matched the railroad's good judgment with his own in his choice of a successor—another Teague (but no relation) and another "colonel" (this time a real one). At the time Henry Teague recruited Arthur S. Teague—whose physician-father was a friend—all the older man knew was that the youth seemed a likely prospect for a summer job on the cog railway. An engineering student at Clemson College in South Carolina, Arthur Teague had planned to begin an eighteen-month General Electric apprenticeship following his graduation. Retrenching to suit the times, General Electric dropped the program. So it was that in 1933, his career plans sidetracked, Arthur Teague came to the cog railway. He stayed there until his death in the summer of 1967, although he took time out to serve in World War II; he entered that conflict as a lieutenant and emerged as a colonel with nearly every decoration for bravery the United States can bestow save the Congressional Medal of Honor.

There were more parallels between the two Teagues than their surnames. Each man brought to the cog railway at the time of his arrival the qualities it most needed to survive. Henry Teague geared the line to the age of autos, motels, and expressways. Arthur Teague, charged with the operation of a railway that could be fairly described as an anachronism in action, brought to the line the engineering and technical knowledge needed to operate it successfully, make needed improvements, and hold the reins on costs. His work evokes memories of Mark Twain's Connecticut Yankee: "I could make anything a body wanted—anything in the world, it didn't make any difference what; and if there wasn't any quick new-fangled way to make a thing, I could invent one."

For example: the cog railway's Base Station is six miles from the nearest electric power line; the necessary connecting links would have cost $20,000. Arthur Teague harnessed falling water on the mountainside to turn a Pelton water wheel that generates electricity for the Base Station, operates all the shop machinery through belt drives, and turns a water motor that pumps water to the

CONTINUED ON PAGE 106

Hugo Black and the

K.K.K.

President Roosevelt had failed to "pack" a hostile Supreme Court, and now the first New Dealer he named to that high bench stood accused of being a lifetime member of the infamous Ku Klux Klan

By VIRGINIA VAN DER VEER

Had it not been for politics, the paths of Franklin Delano Roosevelt and Hugo La Fayette Black might never have crossed. Roosevelt had been born to wealth and to a patrician, manorial legacy in the Hudson River valley. Black came from yeoman stock in rural Alabama, and his birthrights were little more than a keen mind and prodigious energy. But the Democratic party and common political convictions brought these two together, one as the President and the other as a United States senator from Alabama. Now, on the sultry evening of August 11, 1937, they sat facing each other in a cluttered upstairs study in the White House.

After a few pleasantries, Roosevelt came quickly to the point. He would like to place the name of Hugo Black in nomination for a seat on the United States Supreme Court. Holding out an official paper, the President said: "Hugo, I'd like to write your name here." The Senator, forewarned, had talked it over with his wife, who urged him to accept. Receiving the answer he expected, Roosevelt crisply inscribed the words "Hugo L. Black, of Alabama" and sealed the nomination in an envelope.

Secretly, without consulting his usual advisers, Franklin Roosevelt had chosen his first nominee to the Supreme Court. The President evidently felt no need to inquire into the political past of a senator who had so staunchly supported most of his programs. Later, a chagrined Roosevelt would tell his friends that one normally did not ask a man "questions of that sort."

Associate Supreme Court Justice Black, returning from a European vacation, is surrounded on a Norfolk pier by reporters eager to question him about his Klan involvement. Wearing a ten-gallon hat (behind Black) is Ray Sprigle, whose sensational disclosures in the Pittsburgh Post-Gazette *later won him a Pulitzer prize.*

This photograph of the Supreme Court, on which an artist painted a Klan costume over retiring Justice Van Devanter, appeared on page one of the New York Sun *on Saturday, October 2, 1937. The picture bore the following caption: "Front row, left to right—Justice Brandeis, The Former Klansman, Chief Justice Hughes, Justice McReynolds and Justice Sutherland. Rear row, left to right—Justice Roberts, Justice Butler, Justice Stone and Justice Cardozo."*

If Roosevelt had sought the advice of that astute Democratic politician, Postmaster General James A. Farley, he might have been reminded that Hugo Black had entered the Senate with the backing of the Alabama Ku Klux Klan. If the President had talked it over with Charles Michelson, the Democratic ghost writer and former newspaperman, he might have learned of rumors that Black had actually been a member of the Klan.

But neither these men nor any of the Senate leaders knew of Roosevelt's intention. Attorney General Homer S. Cummings was the President's only confidant, and he had made no inquiry into Senator Black's background either. To investigate a man twice elected to the United States Senate, Cummings insisted afterward, would have been an "impertinence."

The President came to his decision in the closing days of a summer session of a Congress whose political debates

61

had been as torrid as the temperature along the banks of the Potomac. The battle over Roosevelt's plan for enlarging (his enemies said "packing") the Supreme Court had ended in defeat for the President on July 22, after one hundred and sixty-eight days of bitter controversy. (See "F. D. R. vs. the Supreme Court" in the April, 1958, AMERICAN HERITAGE.)

For Roosevelt the loss had been costly—in prestige, in his working relationship with the Senate, and in the death of his loyal majority leader, Senator Joseph T. Robinson of Arkansas. Worn out by the strain of trying to hold fractious Democratic ranks together, Robinson, the peacemaker, died at the height of the epic struggle.

Although the game was lost, the President still had one card to play, and he wanted to make it a trump. Justice Willis Van Devanter's decision in May to step down from active service on the court gave Roosevelt an opportunity to name a justice. This first vacancy had long been promised to the conservative Robinson; but with Robinson gone, all options were open to the President.

In choosing Hugo Black, Roosevelt was not thinking of his nominee's political origins or looking for the country's most brilliant legal mind. He wanted to put an ardent New Dealer on the bench of a Supreme Court that had stubbornly bucked the legislative program of his first administration. But would the recalcitrant Senate confirm such a choice? The surest way to guarantee confirmation would be to name one of its own members, since the Senate traditionally confirmed its own.

A list of sixty potential nominees, compiled by the Department of Justice, was gradually whittled down. It would be politically tactful to select a man from an area not represented on the court. The Deep South, a Democratic fief astir with political revolt, was such a region.

Furthermore, southern senators had been leaders in fighting not only the court plan but also the administration's wages-and-hours bill, sponsored in the Senate by Hugo Black. They feared that a national scale of minimum wages and maximum hours would stunt the industrial growth of the South by putting an end to the old southern lures of low wages and a tractable labor force. Voicing this philosophy, Ellison D. "Cotton Ed" Smith of South Carolina told the Senate that conditions in the South were so kindly that one could live "comfortably and reasonably" for fifty cents a day.

Provoked to a rare display of emotion, Senator Black defended his bill against his fellow southerners. "I subscribe," he shouted in the Senate, "to the gospel that a man who is born in Alabama and who can do as much work as a man born in any state in New England is entitled to the same pay if he does the same work." The Black-Connery bill passed the Senate on August 1, only to become stalled in the House. There were few in Wash-

Mr. Justice Black: a posteriori

In the history of the Supreme Court, only seven men have served longer than Hugo La Fayette Black. As this is written (in January, 1968), he is in his thirty-first year on the bench. Few justices have been more consistent in their interpretations of the Constitution and, ironically, more often misread by friend and foe alike. Because he was from Alabama and had once expediently been a member of the Klan, he was called a bigot; because he was a New Dealer in the Senate, he was labelled a radical. He was and is neither. Black is a constitutional libertarian who has steadfastly and at times eloquently supported individual liberties, during a tempestuous court era that has encompassed the New Deal, World War II, McCarthyism, and, most recently, the civil rights revolution. His decisions—usually in dissent at first, and then, as the rest of the court moves in his direction, with the majority—have invariably transcended race, creed, and religion.

Perhaps no other area of the law better illustrates his public dilemma than the question of racism, which caused the furor over his appointment in the beginning. Three years after he joined the court, Black delivered (appropriately, on Lincoln's Birthday) an opinion that upset the convictions for murder of four Florida Negroes based on what he called "sunrise confessions" extracted by the police. President Roosevelt promptly informed the press that it owed Justice Black an apology for having sensationalized the Klan episode.

Similarly, Negro and white liberal groups alike began a painful reappraisal of the Justice that was climaxed in 1954, when Black's persuasive influence was credited with having helped produce a unanimous court in the epic *Brown v. Board of Education* desegregation case.

ington optimistic enough to predict that it would finally become the Fair Labor Standards Act of 1938.

Newspapermen familiar with Roosevelt's moods described the President in those August dog days as "sore and vengeful." He wanted to surprise the Senate and, in particular, to give its rebellious southerners a bitter pill that they would have to swallow. If his nominee pleased the administration's powerful new allies in organized labor, so much the better. Few senators were held in higher esteem by union chieftains than Hugo Black, who had stubbornly pressed since 1932 for labor's dream of a thirty-hour work week.

Obviously, the President's sympathies were also aroused. Black's loyalty to Roosevelt in the court fight and his supposed heresy to the South in the wage-hour controversy had encouraged forces in Alabama that were opposed to his re-election in 1938. Many Alabama newspapers openly demanded Black's defeat. Lumber and industrial interests, fighting the pending labor law, stirred up Alabama farmers with the argument that higher pay in the mills would mean higher prices in the stores.

Weighing all these factors, discarding one by one the other possible nominees, Roosevelt made his choice. "And they'll have to take him, too," he told Farley gleefully, after the news broke.

At noon on August 12, when the White House courier arrived at the door of the Senate, the burden of the Presi- dent's message was known only to Senator and Mrs. Black and Attorney General Cummings. At the White House, Roosevelt, impatient as a small boy with a trick to play, waited for his surprise to be revealed. To see the impact for himself, he shared the news with Press Secretary Stephen T. Early. "Jesus Christ!" exclaimed Early, and the President grinned.

As the White House messenger approached the Senate podium, Black, in a white linen suit, sat quietly at his desk, his face impassive. An observant reporter noted that the Senator held a sheaf of papers, which he was methodically shredding into small bits. From the gallery, Mrs. Black, in a dark suit and broad-brimmed hat, peered anxiously down.

Senator Henry F. Ashurst, chairman of the Judiciary Committee, asked unanimous consent to consider immediately a message from the President. Hiram W. Johnson, the progressive Republican from California who had supported Roosevelt in 1932 and 1936 but had fought against the court plan, asked the nature of the message. Told that it was a Supreme Court nomination, Johnson promptly objected to immediate consideration.

Nevertheless, at the direction of Vice President John Nance Garner, the Senate clerk opened the message and began to read: "I nominate Hugo L. Black. . . ." After a moment of stunned silence, Ashurst rose to plead again for immediate action in accordance with the "immemo-

This, in turn, produced a violent reaction from the South, which branded its native son a traitor. Today, however, the liberal enthusiasm for Black is again waning, in the face of his successful efforts to get the court to uphold certain convictions of civil rights demonstrators. "The right to freedom of expression," Black pointed out in one case, "is a right to express views—not a right to force other people to supply a platform or a pulpit."

Black is now eighty-two. Last year he underwent two operations to remove cataracts so that he can go on reading and working. When I visited him one afternoon recently, he was reading proofs of an article he had written for the Encyclopaedia Britannica on the links between Western civilization and that of ancient Greece. Because of the operations, he was wearing thick lenses, and his desk was surrounded by a bank of bright lights focused on a stack of papers typed in outsized letters.

We talked for a while about the intricacies of Alabama politics and then about his pet idea during the Depression of a thirty-hour work week to spread the jobs around. When I brought up the Klan episode, he said again that he still cannot understand what the fuss was about, since all the information had been published before his appointment. Black said he was surprised to hear that Esdale was alive, and he seemed genuinely interested in my account of the former Grand Dragon's present occupation as a bail bondsman whose clients include many Negroes and civil rights workers.

We had talked almost an hour when the door opened without the formality of a knock. It was Elizabeth, the second Mrs. Black (his first wife, Josephine, died in 1951), fiftyish, attractive, once his secretary and now clearly skillful and devoted in her role as wife. She had come to drive him to some Washington ceremony, but said tactfully that she was early and would wait outside.

The interview was over anyway. The Justice emerged from the circle of lights and walked slowly to the door. His doctors, he remarked candidly, had told him a year before that if he ever stopped playing tennis, even for a few days, he could never start again. But now, he said, they are encouraging him to renew his exercises, and he spoke of hitting the tennis ball around some more soon.

I could still sense the determination and intensity of will that had brought this man from an isolated southern county seat to the nation's highest court. If his step was no longer spry, his mind had lost none of its vitality. I thought, as we shook hands, that if Hugo Black willed it, he would play many another set of tennis.   —*Virginia Van der Veer*

rial usage" of the Senate. But Johnson was adamant. For the first time since 1888, the executive appointment of a senator or former senator was referred to a committee for investigation.

A few of Black's colleagues gathered around to congratulate the nominee, but many others allowed their displeasure to show on their faces. The reporter for the *New York Times* said the nomination of Black "dropped like salt into political wounds already rubbed raw. . . ." Columnist Dorothy Thompson called the choice "cheap," and she added: "We have finally carried the spoils system to the Supreme bench, openly and cynically." But William Allen White wrote in the Emporia, Kansas, *Gazette* that the President had hit a "veritable three-bagger" by naming a liberal, a southerner, and a man whom the Senate would have to confirm.

Black ate lunch alone that day in the Senate restaurant. Even after ten years, he had few friends in the upper chamber. Washington journalists described him as a "loner" and said he suffered from an "unpopularity complex." An ardent partisan in floor debate and a zealous investigator in committee hearings, Black had neither time nor temperament for Senate camaraderie. Committee witnesses and senators alike had felt his withering sarcasm or the quick lash of his tongue. Once, after listening to a three-hour speech by Michigan's Arthur H. Vandenberg, Black arose, complimented Vandenberg, and gravely announced he had only one question to ask: "Is the Senator for or against the bill?"

As a Senate investigator, Black was often compared to the late Thomas J. Walsh of Montana, who had exposed the Elk Hills and Teapot Dome scandals of the Harding administration. Black set out to reveal graft and special privileges—especially during Republican administrations—in government subsidies to airlines and merchant shipping, and later to expose the guises under which lobbyists tried to influence Congress.

In this role he won nationwide attention and set in motion several significant reforms, but his zeal provoked many an unflattering description. One newspaper spoke of his "rhadamanthine eyes," a magazine called him a "useful Torquemada," a fellow senator said he used the methods of the Ogpu, the Soviet secret service, and regulars in the Senate press gallery nicknamed him "the ferret." As a cross-examiner, Black was so rigorous that a shipping-company president called to the witness stand brought along his physician to check his pulse.

In making Black his nominee, then, Roosevelt was rewarding a Senate career of zestful controversy. But there were those in the Senate who remembered its origin. Before the committee hearings began, gossip circulated in the marble corridors about events that had taken place in Alabama more than a decade earlier.

If Hugo Black thought of the Klan at all in 1937, it was as a chapter in his life that was long since closed. In the early 1920's, as a young, politically ambitious lawyer, he liked to describe himself as a "jiner." He taught the largest adult Sunday-school class in Birmingham, and was a Mason, a Knight of Pythias, and an Odd Fellow. On September 11, 1923, in an act of political expediency, Hugo Black took the oath as one of 10,000 members of Robert E. Lee Klan No. 1.

Wartime patriotism had provided an excuse for a rebirth of the old Ku Klux Klan, and, feeding on a postwar surge of bigotry and nativism, it grew powerful. In Alabama in the mid-1920's its membership was estimated at between 85,000 and 95,000. There, as in many other states, the Klan ruled politics. When Oscar W. Underwood, the veteran Alabama senator, dared to oppose the order, Klan leaders vowed to retire him from political life. Birmingham Klansmen, initiating some 7,000 new Knights in an outdoor ceremony in 1924, cheered as a coffin containing an effigy of Underwood was "laid to rest" through a trap door in the speakers' platform. Foreseeing defeat, Underwood chose not to seek re-election.

Two years later, supported by the Klan and the prohibitionists, Hugo Black, forty years of age and relatively unknown, swept past four prominent Alabama politicians to win the Senate nomination in the Democratic primary, thus virtually assuring his election. For more than a year he had campaigned in every county of the state, wearing out two cars on the dusty rural roads.

To forestall criticism of a candidate who was a Klan member, Black had prudently submitted his resignation before he began to campaign. But after his primary victory, he openly acknowledged that Klan support—more than his own energy—had won him the nomination. Speaking to a state-wide Klan rally, he thanked Klansmen and told them he was aware that, without their help, he would not be a United States senator.

Some newspapers drew the same conclusion. The *New York Times* attributed to Klan support the nominations of Black to the Senate and Bibb Graves to the Alabama governorship. The Montgomery *Advertiser* called Black "the darling of the Klan," and the Birmingham *News* quoted the state's Klan leader, rejoicing at the election returns: "We licked 'em clean."

But the Klan died out as an effective political force, and by 1930 Senator Black had openly broken his ties with it. He was re-elected in 1932, with remnants of the order opposing him. By 1937 the genesis of Black's Senate career, once a familiar political yarn in Alabama, was half-forgotten.

The Supreme Court nomination resurrected it. Despite the rumors, however, the nomination of Hugo Black moved smoothly through a subcommittee, the only

CONTINUED ON PAGE 108

HOW TO SALT A GOLD MINE

By DAVID LAVENDER

In the mining country
of the Old West some men
struck it rich without
touching a shovel.
All it took was a little
legerdemain—and a sucker
bitten by the gold bug

ILLUSTRATED FOR AMERICAN HERITAGE BY GERRY GERSTEN

A classic western aphorism commonly attributed to Mark Twain defines a gold or silver mine as a hole in the ground with a liar on top. Generally, the misrepresentations were a standard form of mining-camp bragging—but not always. Luxurious rewards awaited the bunco artist who could make gold seem to appear in a hole where no gold actually existed, or the con man who could produce, for suspicious examining engineers, specimens of silver that assayed higher (as the gulled buyer discovered too late) than the ore body from which they supposedly came.

Small investments could produce grand returns. By dishonestly increasing the apparent per-ton worth by a mere twenty-five cents, a seller could unload a hundred-thousand-ton mine for $25,000 above its value. Microscopic amounts of metal were enough to create such inflation. Dusting a ton of ore with one eightieth of an ounce of gold, at its price of $20.67 per ounce, would add twenty-five cents to the value per ton—as would less than one quarter of an ounce of silver.

Nor was it necessary to sprinkle the salt, as the fraudulent additive was called, throughout the exposed ore—that would have been too expensive—but only in those samples, taken here and there, from which the valuation of the mine was calculated. Since many a mine has been sold on the basis of samples totalling only a few tons, less than a hundred dollars might be enough to turn a handsome trick.

Newcomers, panting with desire for quick money, were so convinced that riches could be plucked carrotlike from the ground that they often believed any encouraging signs they saw. And, of course, there were obliging souls ready to provide attractive sights.

No one was handier at furnishing these tantalizing glimpses at high-value ore than William Lovell, champion fraud of Leadville, Colorado, during that famed silver camp's first frantic boom. From the outset, Lovell used more than a pick and shovel to bring him fortune. When he joined the headlong rush across blizzard-swept South Park and over the snow-heaped Mosquito Range in the winter of 1877–78, he took along a wagonload of chickens to sell at premium prices. A howling storm snowed him in near an abandoned log cabin. Freighters who broke through the road several days later found him hale and fat, surrounded by feathers and frozen chicken remains. Ever afterward he was called Chicken Bill.

Bill was one of the first to prospect on Fryer Hill, immediately north of the new camp at Leadville, but he was not as lucky as two Germans, August Rische and George Hook, who followed close behind him. In April of 1878, Rische and Hook obtained a grubstake, including a jug of whisky, from Leadville's storekeeper-mayor, H. A. W. Tabor. The long, back-packing trudge up Fryer Hill winded them. They sat down in the shade of an evergreen, refreshed themselves with a nip from the jug, and looked up the slope ahead. Why climb higher? They started to dig where they were. Twice they ran out of food and had to go back and beg Tabor for more. All told, they used up fifty-four dollars' worth of supplies.

In May, when their shaft was thirty feet deep, they ran into a fabulous vein later known as the Little Pittsburgh. By sheer chance they had hit its apex, the only point where the vein could have been reached with pick and shovel. The first wagonload of ore netted them two hundred dollars. Word spread instantaneously, and Leadville's boom soared. Although Rische and Hook sold their one-third interests in the mine for relatively modest sums (Hook got $98,000 and Rische, selling a little later, $273,000), Tabor held on to his grubstake third for a year. He netted $500,000 in dividends and then sold out for a million. Visitors were understandably impressed.

Immediately after the discovery of the Little Pittsburgh, Tabor quite naturally began buying claims all over the slope. One night, Chicken Bill Lovell stole a few hundred pounds of ore from the Little Pittsburgh and dumped the haul into the barren bottom of his own shaft. He then invited Tabor to look at his

mine. A glance at ore showing *those* characteristics was enough for Leadville's overnight tycoon. Grandly, he gave Bill about $900 for the property.

Wages then ran roughly $2.50 a day, and Bill probably equated the sale with a year's work—not bad. But Tabor may not have been gullible so much as canny. He named his purchase the Chrysolite and had his men sink a shaft through the salted ore and into the rock beneath. They soon hit another vein. Tabor took an estimated $150,000 from it before selling out.

Chicken Bill's next victims were more typical—two English tourists he met one day on the porch of a Leadville hotel. Learning that Lovell was a miner (he did have a few holes scattered here and there, just in case), they plied him with so many questions that he decided to rig a show. The next day, as he was again yarning with the pair on the porch, a pack train shuffled by, the mules loaded with bulging ore sacks.

"From my mine," said Chicken Bill, with an off-hand wave. "Would you like a souvenir?"

The Englishmen said they would. Bill halted the mule drover and opened two sacks, apparently at random. He gave each man a chunk of shiny ore and then ambled off to keep an appointment, so he said.

The tourists rushed to an assayer and had the ore appraised. Eureka! Hoping to outfox Bill, they learned the location of his mine and wandered out to see it —mere tourist curiosity, of course. The hole didn't look like much, but at its mouth was a small pile of that fancy ore, which Bill was busily sacking.

He was grumpy when interrupted. No, he was not interested in selling the mine. Could they look inside? Well, yes, if they were careful not to hurt themselves. He remained outside (proof of his indifference), and when the pair reached the breast of the tunnel they hurriedly knocked off some specimens and hid them in their pockets. Being greenhorns, they took the pieces that broke off most readily—too readily, in fact, for Bill had just placed them there.

Assays of those pieces also revealed a high silver content. After earnest entreaties, the gulls managed to persuade Bill to part with the property. And this claim did not backfire, as the Chrysolite had: it stayed barren, while Bill settled down contentedly to another year of paid-up existence. Since he had never *offered* to sell them the mine, the English dupes did not risk ridicule by taking the case to court.

Chicken Bill became so famous as a salter that he even received credit, possibly undeserved, for creating a stampede to the western shoulder of Pikes Peak in 1884. What happened, apparently, was that trade was languishing in the nearby railroad town of Cañon

City. Hoping to revive it, certain merchants paid two Leadville ne'er-do-wells, S. J. Bradley and D. G. Miller, two hundred dollars to dig a hole eighteen feet deep on a slope forty-five miles from Canon City, and to produce, supposedly from that hole, ore that assayed at $2,000 a ton. The scheme worked. Five thousand people poured into Canon City, swarming through the hotels, hardware stores, groceries, and livery stables, buying supplies for prospecting trips. When trained miners showed their suspicions, the salters vanished. Because local gossip had it that Bradley had once worked for William Lovell in Leadville, Chicken Bill was thought to have had a hand in the business, and he still appears in some history books as the perpetrator of the great Mount Pisgah hoax. If so, he must have had even wrier memories about it than about the Chrysolite, for a few years later gold *was* found at Mount Pisgah. The field developed into Cripple Creek, maker of at least twenty-eight millionaires.

Methods like Chicken Bill's of introducing outside ore into a mine he proposed to sell were essentially crude—success depended on the greed of the buyer. When there was greed, almost any device worked. Consider, for instance, the incredible brashness of one salter during the early frenzies on Nevada's Comstock Lode. He simply scattered a few handfuls of cut-up silver half dollars throughout the broken rock in the bottom of his shaft. A prospective buyer chemically treated, milled, and amalgamated several tons of the "ore." Dazzled by the returns, the buyer all but sprained his wrist reaching for his checkbook and did not learn the truth until, on starting his own operation, he discovered a battered coin lodged in a crevice.

Undeveloped prospect holes such as these seldom sold for high prices. A Chicken Bill might be content with a return of a thousand dollars or so, but big-money frauds preferred to work with mines whose various shafts and drifts had penetrated enough veins to suggest ore bodies of truly majestic scale. A type of property especially favored for salting was one that had started as a bonanza operation but whose vein was threatening to turn barren as the depth increased.

If this drop in value could be hidden from potential buyers, then a sale at a highly satisfying figure—satisfying to the seller, at least—might be achieved.

Investors risking $100,000 or more seldom bought such a property without first seeking the advice of trained engineers. Mine sampling, as the engineers' investigations are called, developed into a complex skill whose rudiments were taught in engineering schools. Although accurate evaluation of the mine rather than detection of fraud was the sampler's main purpose, gigantic swindles became so common that textbooks on mining still outline the basic tricks.

The principles of sampling were routine enough. The engineer, generally assisted by a reliable crew, cut a widely spaced series of shallow grooves, an inch or two deep and four or five inches wide, across as much of the vein as had been exposed. The chips from each groove were individually sacked in stout canvas bags. The sacks were wired shut, sealed with a lead seal bearing the examiner's "brand," and numbered according to location. Each sackful was then assayed and the mine's potential value calcuated.

Chipping samples out of rock with a hammer and moil, or even with a pneumatic drill, is devilishly hard work, especially when a man has to stand on a rickety scaffold and swing over his head at the roof of a stope, as excavations in the vein are called. Nevertheless, precautions are taken to assure accurate samples. Clean canvas is spread to prevent adulteration from rock scattered on the ground.

Matters are further complicated by the fact that values are seldom evenly distributed throughout a vein. Most ores are friable and full of cracks. Fine dust carrying above-average concentrations of metal is likely to collect in these cracks. Because cracked ore breaks loose fairly readily, a lazy or careless engineer, intending no fraud whatsoever, may wind up with a sampling far richer than the mine will bear out. Results can be disastrous.

One famous example of this sort of unintentional salting occurred at the Ray copper mine in south-central Arizona in 1899. A careless English engineer let his Mexican crew collect samples without adequate supervision. They naturally chipped away at the softest spots. The samples, sent to London for assaying, indicated a bonanza—rock containing five per cent copper, or a hundred pounds of metal per ton. Excited investors built a railroad into the area, erected a mill, and built tennis courts, a golf links, and a polo field to go with houses staffed with butlers who astounded the local populace by serving afternoon tea.

Repeated mill runs on the first 50,000 tons of ore showed that the samples had erred by about two per cent. Within two years the company was bankrupt. More cautious American investors took over the operation a few years later and spent $300,000 to sample the mine. Eventually mass-production techniques and an ore body of over a hundred million tons made the Ray mine one of America's greatest producers.

As engineers became more sophisticated, so did swindlers. Some bunco artists tamped minute fillings of dental gold into tiny cavities in the rock. Others preferred to paint the face of the ore bed with a solution of gold chloride or silver nitrate, as the case might be, or to squirt the liquid into cracks with a syringe. Another favorite device was to load a shotgun shell with coin shavings and fire the charge at close range against the rock. Enough metal adhered to give high assay values to samples chipped from that face.

But these methods did not go undetected. Suspicious engineers vigorously washed down the rock faces with brush and water, or blasted a foot or so of rock off the face and sampled the freshly exposed ore before a salter could get at it. Frustrated by these precautions, the salters then turned with fresh ingenuity to meddling with the samples themselves.

Gold dust is easily concealed in any kind of tobacco. Doctored quids were sometimes used by the sellers of California placer mines. A man would bite off a chew, chomp it well, and spit into the pool of water he was using for washing the gravel in his gold pan. Inevitably the residue showed colors.

Ashes from the pipes of native women employed on the sluicing operations at the head of the Jaina River in the Dominican Republic salted those alluvial deposits enough to bleed thousands of dollars from a Boston mining concern. Subsequently, an American con man named Ely Dorsey got hold of the same Jaina River field and interested some Philadelphia capital in running extensive boring, panning, and sluicing tests. Values were intriguing—thanks to tiny clay pills, each containing a grain of gold, dropped into the

David Lavender is the author of the American Heritage History of the Great West. *His most recent article in the magazine itself was* How to Make it to the White House Without Really Trying *in June of last year.*

gravel by native workers. No sale resulted, however, because suspicions were properly aroused when five of the workers suddenly disappeared.

Before long, no engineer would allow tobacco users near a place where sampling was going on. Nor were workers allowed to wear their fingernails long. Wax under the nails of one bribed Mexican laborer in western Chihuahua enabled him to transfer tiny flakes of gold from his pockets to some samples, and his employer extracted a down payment on the mine of $100,000 from a San Francisco operator.

Toward the close of the last century, churn drills were introduced for sampling ore bodies hundreds of feet beneath the surface of the earth. A heavy drilling bit on the end of a stem was lifted a few feet by a cable run by a steam engine on the surface. The bit was then dropped back into the hole. The chips loosened by this hammering accumulated in the water that was dribbled into the hole to soften the earth. Every so often the sludge was raised to the surface, dried, and assayed. Engineer C. S. Haley told, in a 1913 issue of the *Mining and Scientific Press,* of a test hole that he carefully sealed against tampering during nights when the crew was away. Nevertheless, the hole was salted. The swindler did it by sprinkling gold dust into mud that he then smeared onto the cable attached to the bit. The next morning the dried mud jiggled loose as the cable moved up and down; the mud fell to the bottom of the hole and raised the apparent values. But one morning the swindler applied the mud too late. An alert driller wondered why fresh mud was on a cable that had been idle all night. The plot failed.

Salters were unfazed by canvas sample sacks with their wired-shut mouths and lead seals. Sometimes they got hold of the bags before they were used, and sprinkled grains of gold along the fuzzy inside seams. Some managed to take wax impressions of the engineer's seals, make duplicates, open and salt the sacks at leisure, and reseal them with the counterfeit seals. Or, given the proper circumstances, they would slit the bags open, salt them, and sew them up again.

Refined swindlers occasionally blew gold dust into sample sacks through goose quills, or injected solutions of gold chloride with hypodermic needles. One suspicious engineer, investigating a mine on an island near Juneau, Alaska (selling price: $450,000), demanded that the owners and their men leave the island while he did his sampling. He took his sample sacks to the docks at Juneau and hired watchmen to guard them night and day until a ship arrived that would take them to San Francisco for assaying. During the wait, dudes would wander by on various occasions asking foolish questions of the bored watchmen and now and then poking at the sacks with their walking sticks. Many weeks later the buyers figured out that there must have been syringes in the ends of those canes. By then, however, it was too late. The deal had gone through, and the victims were stuck.

The equipment in an assayer's office—crushers, mortars, crucibles, and the like—could also be doctored, sometimes without the assayer's collusion, but more often with it. Furthermore, an occasional assayer was a friendly soul who liked to report pleasantly high values in order to keep business coming—and some miners, like some health-seekers, will keep looking for a diagnostician who will tell them what they want to hear. Mark Twain, in *Roughing It,* described how one such assayer at Virginia City, Nevada, was exposed when suspicious rivals sent him a fragment from a carpenter's grindstone; the assayer said he found both silver and gold in it. More than half a century later, a skeptical, well-read California engineer trapped a fraudulent assayer in San Diego by exactly the same device—chips from a grindstone that the assayer declared to be worth fifteen dollars a ton in gold.

According to experienced engineers, salting cannot be absolutely prevented; the most a prospective buyer can hope for is that he will detect the fraud in time. One way is to invert the process by placing dummy sacks of barren rock among the legitimate samples. If the worthless specimens suddenly blossom with gold or silver, something is amiss and the buyer is well advised to quietly drop his options. In such cases there is not much use in trying to prove fraud against any particular individual. The best one can do is to sit tight, growl though he may. Perhaps that is why the following tale from Yreka, California, is so gratifying.

In the old days, Chinese were often barred from California placer operations until after the whites had moved on. Then, with extreme patience and endless labor, the Orientals managed to rework the sifted ground at a profit. Hence, they were willing to pay for claims that showed any trace of gold at all. Hearing that a certain Chinaman was shopping around Yreka for claims, and was talking in terms of $5,000, two salters rushed to their abandoned holdings, sprinkled five hundred dollars' worth of gold dust in the gravel, and let the Oriental test it. He admitted to finding color, but asked for time to make up his mind. The extension was granted, but at its end the buyer did not appear. The light began to dawn, and the would-be sellers hastened to their property. Sure enough, the scoundrel had carefully washed their five hundred dollars' worth of salt out of the gravel and had vanished—perhaps to pull the trick on over-eager swindlers somewhere else.

Would You Believe

By SAMUEL CARTER III

Salted Salt Water?

There is, as everyone knows, more than one kind of fish in the sea. And, as some bunco artists will tell some poor fish, there is more than fish in sea water.

Near the turn of the present century, Prescott Ford Jernegan, a respected Baptist minister from Edgartown, Massachusetts, claimed that a dream had revealed to him the way to extract gold from the ocean. The process involved passing an electrical current through a submerged, zinc-lined wooden box (an "accumulator") containing chemically treated quicksilver. The gold was supposedly absorbed by the mercury.

A pair of wealthy parishioners, A. B. Ryan and A. N. Pierson, had a box constructed to Jernegan's specifications. Jernegan hired Charles Fisher, a deep-sea diver who later became his partner, to submerge and connect the device for preliminary testing. Then, on a cold February night in 1897, Ryan and Pierson themselves lowered the box into Narragansett Bay. After a full running of the tide they hauled it up. Government assayers found five dollars' worth of pure gold—not sensational but promising, promising.

Ryan, Pierson, Jernegan, and two others put up $20,000 for a more extensive test at a remote inlet near Lubec, Maine. Some of the investors were sure they had another Klondike. In December of 1897 they formed the Electrolytic Marine Salts Company, capitalized at ten million dollars. "Mining" operations were centered at Lubec, but the company's headquarters were set up in Boston. Wealthy eastern Baptists bought most of the first 350,000 shares. Within six months another 350,000 were issued and snapped up. There were now 250 accumulators yielding $1,250 each turn of the tide. The firm made well-publicized

Mr. Carter, author of the recently published Cyrus Field: Man of Two Worlds, *lives in Wakefield, R. I.*

70

shipments of gold every week to New York City.

Jernegan declined to get a patent, maintaining, among other things, that sea water was public domain. He preferred to rely on secrecy: only he and Fisher, who remained in charge at Lubec, knew the formula.

There were skeptics, but even the press was guarded in its comments. Gold was known to be in suspension in sea water, and others had worked to try to get it out. Maybe Jernegan *had* hit on the right method.

The clincher came when a dubious Boston investment counselor named Tibbetts hired a chemist, one Dr. Carmichael, to investigate. Picking an accumulator at random, Carmichael demanded that salt water be scooped up at a spot he designated. Jernegan said that the process required a continual flow. "Use your hand to stir the water," said Carmichael, "and keep it *open*." The clergyman complied. At his laboratory, Carmichael analyzed the contents and found gold.

Lubec boomed. The firm now had 700 workmen; the goal was 10,000 accumulators and an annual potential of $17,500,000.

But there were hitches and suspicions. A workman was found murdered. Then, one day in July of 1898, the accumulators were found damaged and disconnected—and Fisher had vanished. Jernegan said he thought Fisher had fled to Europe to open his own plant. He offered to go after him.

Jernegan's share in the operation was forty-five per cent of the proceeds from the sale of the stock. Soon after he left, it was discovered that he had withdrawn most of some $300,000 he had stashed in various banks and that he had carefully paid his debts. There was one man, however, who claimed that Jernegan owed him money, and he gave his story to the press.

William Phelan said that he had been hired to help Fisher, who, he said, had salted the boxes with scrap gold that travelled a continuous triangle—from the accumulators to New York to a secret room in Fisher's house and back to the accumulators. As public skepticism had waned, said Phelan, it had been necessary to salt just a few boxes, to meet unpredictable investigations.

Hoping to maintain a surprisingly unshaken public confidence, Jernegan sent $85,000 from Paris to help repair the boxes and resume operations, but when letters between him and Fisher were uncovered, the hoax was confirmed and Phelan's story substantiated.

Jernegan returned to America, and a court case held that the returned $85,000 had left him with only the forty-five per cent of stock sales he was entitled to. He was free, but his reputation was ruined—and he was apparently broke. He disappeared and eventually died in Manila. Fisher's obituary appeared in an Australian newspaper in 1900. Some thought he had written and planted it himself. The Lubec plant was sold (it became a cannery producing Klondyke brand finnan haddie); Electrolytic stockholders got thirty-five cents on the dollar.

Again and again Tibbetts and Carmichael went over the hoax. Where had they been tripped up? Finally Tibbetts had a thought: When Jernegan stirred the water, had he been wearing a ring? Come to think of it, he had—a gold ring, traces of which had dissolved in the mercury.

But what of the money Jernegan had taken to Europe? While there, as he later confided to his family, he had heard of a similar gold-from-sea-water scheme in England. He had invested everything he had in it—and had been swindled.

but the *Monocacy* had damaged herself on a submerged rock and was leaking badly. The American vessels steamed back down the river and rejoined the main fleet, where the sound of the cannonading had aroused much alarm.

Rodgers and Low were incensed by the attack on their ships. It was, they felt, an act of premeditated treachery, a deliberate affront to the flag that they could not and would not ignore. Accordingly they sent word to the Korean government (by attaching a message to a stake on Guerrière Island) that unless it apologized within ten days there would be armed reprisal. At the same time Rodgers ordered preparations made for an amphibious assault on Kanghoa Island.

Both the Admiral and the Minister were of the opinion that, in Low's words, "It is mistaken policy when dealing with oriental governments and peoples to allow insults and injuries to go unredressed. Such leniency leads them to believe that fear alone prevents retaliation, and adds to their arrogance, conceit, and hostility." He and Rodgers further believed that retaliation would not lessen the chances of negotiation but instead might actually improve them, for (again to quote Low) "evidences were multiplying that all our overtures made in a conciliatory spirit would be peremptorily rejected."

Five days later, on June 7, a junk approached the *Colorado* and a messenger came aboard with two letters in Chinese, one from the King, the other from the governor of Kanghoa Island. The first (which was a copy of a communication sent to Low via the Chinese, but which he had not received prior to leaving Peking) denied that the Koreans had been at fault in the *General Sherman* affair, cited several instances in which they had aided shipwrecked American sailors, and declared that nonintercourse with foreigners was the immutable policy of the land.

The governor's letter, far from apologizing for the attack on the survey fleet, asserted that the commander of the forts had simply done his duty, for "when your honorable vessels, not considering the fixed regulations of another country, penetrated its important pass, how could the officers, appointed to guard the portals of the frontier . . . calmly let it go by as of no consequence?" The governor closed by expressing concern that the Americans might be hungry after "a voyage of 10,000 *li* of wind and wave," and offered "as a trifling assistance to your table" three bullocks, fifty chickens, and ten thousand eggs.

Rodgers angrily denounced the governor's message as "insulting" and refused to accept the proffered gifts.

Low did not even consider it worthy of an answer.

And thus it was that late on the morning of June 10 the *Monocacy*, the *Palos*, and the four steam launches again began puffing their way up the river. The *Palos* had in tow twenty longboats packed with a landing party of 546 sailors and 105 marines equipped with Remington breech-loading carbines and seven howitzers. Besides its regular armament, the *Monocacy* mounted two nine-inch guns from the *Colorado*. Again Blake was in over-all command of the operation, which had as its objective the destruction of all fortifications on Kanghoa Island. He and his men were confident that soon they would give the Koreans a "good drubbing" and then "kick their mud forts down the hill."

At 1 P.M. the *Monocacy* began shelling the southernmost fort on the island. Its garrison quickly fled, and American marines and sailors, headed by Commander Lewis A. Kimberly, splashed ashore. To their dismay they found themselves wallowing up to their knees, even to their waists, in the slimy goo of the mud flat. Cursing and sweating, losing their shoes and ripping their trousers, they struggled across to firm land, a dozen men being needed to drag, sometimes literally to carry, each howitzer. They then pushed on and occupied the abandoned fort, where they spent the rest of the day destroying the Korean installations.

Meanwhile the *Monocacy* proceeded farther upstream and opened fire on the "middle" fort. This time the Koreans responded vigorously with their artillery, but did no damage other than to cut some rigging. The *Monocacy* continued to pound the fort, until nightfall caused it to break off the engagement. The *Palos*, while moving to support her sister ship, ran aground on an unseen rock. Not until the next day, and only after much difficulty, did she get off, taking water through a bad gash in her hull.

Kimberly established two camps, one for his sailors near the captured fort, the other some distance away for his marines. Toward midnight, hundreds of Korean troops, ghostlike in the summer darkness, approached the camps, howling, beating drums, and firing wildly. A few salvos from the howitzers scattered them, and they did not come back.

At dawn the *Monocacy* resumed shelling the middle fort. At the same time, Kimberly's column approached it up the riverbank. Fearful of being cut off, the defenders fled without firing a shot. They left behind sixty loaded cannons—all brass breechloaders with two-inch bores. Kimberly detailed a work party to tumble these ridiculous pieces into the river, and with the bulk of his force moved on to attack the main fort at the northern end of the island.

This was a much more formidable fortification than the ones already so easily taken. The Americans called it "the Citadel." It crowned a steep hill 150 feet high and mounted 143 guns. Moreover, it was garrisoned by the elite of the Korean army—the "Tiger Hunters." These were men from the Yalu River region, each of whom had killed at least one tiger singlehandedly, and all of whom were sworn to fight to the death. Flapping above the fort was the huge yellow "General Commanding" banner.

Kimberly's men marched under a blazing sun across a series of hills and ravines. Several times they had to halt while pioneering parties levelled and widened the trail, cut down bushes, or filled in hollows. Whole companies were needed to pull the howitzers, sometimes being forced to lower them into gorges, then haul them out on the other side. Several marines and sailors fainted from heat and exhaustion; others became ill.

As they neared the Citadel, Korean troops began massing on their left. Kimberly at once detached about a third of his force and five howitzers to counter this threat. The rest of the column, under the immediate command of Lieutenant Commander Silas Casey, then took up an assault position in a ravine at the bottom of the hill on which the Citadel stood. Just as they did so, the Koreans outside the fort charged. But, as before, the howitzers quickly smashed their ranks and they made no further attacks.

All that time the *Monocacy,* steaming up the river abreast of the landing party, had been bombarding the Citadel. Now Kimberly's howitzers joined in, lobbing their projectiles right on top of the Korean works. After an hour the fort's cannons no longer replied. Kimberly thereupon signalled the *Monocacy* to cease firing and Casey ordered his men, who had been blazing away at the fort with their rifles, to charge.

They rose with a yell and surged up the hillside, officers in front. A hail of metal from musket and cannon met them, but most of the missiles passed harmlessly over their heads, as the defenders were unable to depress their artillery pieces low enough to take proper aim. The Tiger Hunters, realizing they did not have time to reload, then threw down their muskets and mounted the parapet, swords and spears in hand, chanting a blood-curdling war song; some, in desperation, even threw stones at the onrushing bluecoats.

Lieutenant Hugh W. McKee was the first to enter the fort. Immediately he was struck by a bullet in the groin and a Korean thrust a spear into his thigh. His assailant then lunged at Lieutenant Commander Winfield Scott Schley. The spear pierced Schley's left sleeve, pinning it to his coat. A moment later Schley shot the Korean down. (Schley survived and later became an admiral and the controversial commander of the "Flying Squadron" in the Battle of Santiago de Cuba during the Spanish-American War.)

A fierce hand-to-hand struggle took place inside the fort, carbines and cutlasses opposing swords and spears. Many of the Tiger Hunters wore cotton armor nine layers thick and could be stopped only by bullets fired at close range. On the other hand, their swords were

The Asiatic Squadron at Nagasaki before sailing for Korea. Admiral Rodgers' flagship was the Colorado *(foreground).*

MONOCACY   BENICIA   JUNO   COLORADO   PALOS   OCEAN

made of such soft iron that on contact with the American sabers they bent instead of cutting. All the defenders fought with fanatical courage until killed or badly wounded; not one surrendered voluntarily. In a number of instances weaponless Koreans even scooped up gravel and threw it into the faces of the Americans. The few small groups who did try to escape were mowed down "like rabbits" by detachments Casey had posted outside the fort.

In the end about a hundred surviving Tiger Hunters fled down the hill to the river, where they drowned themselves or cut their own throats; among the latter was the commanding general. At 12:45 P.M. Private Hugh Purvis, U.S.M.C., cut down the generalissimo's large yellow flag and ran up the Stars and Stripes. The battle was over.

Piles of crumpled, white-clad corpses lay in and around the Citadel. Fires had broken out, and there was a sickening smell of burning flesh. Many of the Korean wounded, rather than surrender, silently suffered living cremation. An American sailor, distressed by this scene of horror, asked Marine Captain Tilton for permission to spare the badly wounded by shooting them in the head; Tilton replied that this would be murder and that he must let them remain as they were. In all about 350 Tiger Hunters died in the fighting, and only twenty, all of them wounded, were taken prisoner. The victors' losses, on the other hand, consisted only of McKee and two others killed, and ten wounded. As so often before and since, unsurpassable bravery had proved no match for equal courage supported by superior weapons and tactics.

Kimberly's men remained on the island until the following morning, levelling the fortifications to the ground, burying the dead, and proudly posing for photographs. They then re-embarked and, their boats crammed with trophies, returned with the rest of the expedition to the anchorage, where booming cannons and ringing cheers welcomed them back.

The capture of Kanghoa opened the way to Seoul, but Rodgers had neither the means nor the authority to seize the capital. Moreover, it soon became obvious that the Koreans had not been chastened. When Rodgers offered to return the prisoners, the local governor replied contemptuously: "Do as you please with them." He put them ashore, therefore, to meet whatever fate befell those who, according to the Korean fighting code, were considered already dead.

The plain fact of the matter was that the loss of a few hundred troops meant nothing to the Seoul government. Indeed the loss of the capital itself, as long as the King was safe, would not have been particularly disturbing. Three hundred years before, the Japanese had occupied the entire peninsula but in the end had been forced to evacuate it. The same fate, the Koreans were confident, would befall these new invaders should they persist.

The Americans remained three more weeks at the mouth of the Han, vaguely hoping that the Koreans might even yet agree to negotiations, and making needed repairs on the *Palos* and the *Monocacy*. "We are heartily sick of this place," wrote Captain Tilton to his wife on June 27. "The weather here is enough to give anyone the horrors. It is raining, blowing & fog over everything, and quite uncomfortably close...." Finally, on July 3, the fleet raised anchor and set sail for China. A little over a month later, the first official accounts of what the New York *Herald* headlined as "Our Little War With the Heathen" appeared in the press. The curious public read of the fighting on Kanghoa Island, looked up "Corea" in their atlases, and then turned to the other interesting news of the day—Ku Klux Klan outrages in the South, the illness of Queen Victoria at Balmoral, and yachting at Newport. After all, Korea was far away, and it was not of real consequence to the United States—Seward, Fish, and the China merchants notwithstanding.

But in Korea, a hermit kingdom still, the departure of the barbarian ships was an occasion of great rejoicing and—this would have astonished Rodgers and his men—celebrations of victory. For since the Americans had not succeeded in establishing any meaningful contact with responsible Korean officials, the Koreans believed that the foreigners had merely come to avenge the deaths of pirates and robbers (the crew of the *General Sherman*), but had been so discouraged by the fierce resistance of the Tiger Hunters that they had gone home and would never disturb their land again. Hence the regent had a monument erected in the center of Seoul to commemorate the defeat of the "Western Barbarians." And when, a few years later, a Scottish missionary tried to convince a native of the military superiority of the West, he was answered with a snap of the fingers, "What care we for your foreign inventions? Even our boys laugh at all your weapons!"

Conceived by Seward, ordered by Fish, and headed by Rodgers and Low, the American expedition had been an attempt to do in Korea what Perry had done in Japan eighteen years earlier. Like most imitations, it failed. Not only did Korea remain closed, but its rulers were strengthened in their isolationist policy by the illusion of military victory over the despised Westerners. Of course it could be claimed in the United States, as indeed it was, that the honor of the flag had been upheld; but doubt must be expressed that the one-sided slaughter of poorly armed natives truly accomplished that end.

Essentially, America's first Korean "war" was the tragic consequence of the mutual ignorance and reciprocal arrogance that have so often characterized contacts between East and West. To be sure, Rodgers and Low made mistakes, particularly in sending the survey expedition up the Han without a more definite assurance that it would not provoke an attack; and they might well have displayed less belligerence and more flexibility in dealing with the Koreans. But not all the fault, obviously, was on their side; it is doubtful that any other Americans of the time would have acted differently than these two able men, who had been given a mission which probably was hopeless from the start. When Perry's "black ships" sailed into Tokyo Bay, internal conditions in Japan were ripe for an end to isolationism; in Korea eighteen years later they were not: China, which in the final analysis held the key to Korea, preferred in 1871 to keep the door closed.

Eleven years after Rodgers' sailors and marines stormed the Citadel, another American naval officer, Commodore Robert W. Shufeldt, went to Korea. He had no gunboats or landing parties—only patience, understanding, and tact. With these, and aided by a more conciliatory attitude on the part of the Seoul regime and a diplomatic helping hand from the Chinese (whose policy regarding Korea had in the meantime changed), he made a commercial treaty which for the first time opened "the Land of the Morning Calm" to the Western world.

Unfortunately, Korea soon came under an oppressive Japanese domination, which in turn gave way in 1945 to an unnatural division between a Communist north and a Nationalist south. As a consequence, American fighting men returned to the banks of the Han River, this time not to open up Korea but to prevent it from again being sealed off completely from the West. Once more Americans did battle against Koreans—but struggling bravely by their side were other Koreans who, like those of 1871, were prepared to die rather than succumb to an alien way of life. In history things change; they also remain the same.

Both Dr. Castel and Dr. Nahm are members of the history department of Western Michigan University at Kalamazoo. This is Dr. Castel's third appearance in AMERICAN HERITAGE; a Kansan, he was formerly a Civil War specialist but has recently widened his field of study. Dr. Nahm was born in Pyongyang, Korea (where, incidentally, the General Sherman was destroyed), and has written many articles and monographs on the history of his native country.

Major sources for this article include Corea, The Hermit Nation, by William Elliott Griffis (Scribner, 1904); Homer B. Hulbert's History of Korea, Volume II, revised by Clarence Norwood Weems (Hillary, 1962); and Americans in Eastern Asia, by Tyler Dennett (Barnes & Noble, 1963). Captain Tilton's letters to his wife are to be found in "Marine Amphibious Landing in Korea, 1871," a pamphlet compiled by the Marine Corps's Historical Branch and published in 1966 by the Naval Historical Foundation in Washington.

Butler the Beast? CONTINUED FROM PAGE 53

ject to confiscation. Since human contrabands could no longer be held captive, they were free. The General's adroit legalism became a practical means of destroying slavery long before President Lincoln felt able to issue his formal proclamation. "Contraband of war" became a Northern catch phrase, bringing Butler the hearty applause of the abolitionists.

Butler's military reputation had reached its high-water mark, for his first operation out of Fortress Monroe turned into the North's first rout. In a promising beginning, he took the military post of Newport News, but in mid-June he sent two regiments under the command of another Massachusetts political general, Ebenezer Pierce, up the Peninsula against the Confederate stronghold at Big Bethel. Marching in the darkness, the two units fired upon each other; then, neglecting to send out scouts, they wandered within

point-blank range of Rebel batteries. Butler's troops broke and ran. Big Bethel shattered Northern visions of a quickly-put-down rebellion. Butler blamed Pierce. The country blamed Butler.

Later that summer, Butler engineered a minor amphibious success at Pamlico Sound; this, in the dismal aftermath of Bull Run, was magnified into a great Union victory. Lincoln gratefully gave Butler a leave of absence to raise more troops in New England for Flag Officer David Farragut's amphibious expedition against New Orleans.

The South considered New Orleans, its largest and wealthiest city, to be impregnable. Seventy miles to the south of it lay Forts Jackson and St. Philip, guarding the approaches along the Mississippi. Nevertheless, Farragut and Commander David Porter sailed past the forts by night in April of 1862; New Orleans fell. Butler's army of occupation arrived without firing a shot.

The General rode through sullen streets and heard jeers that he would never see his home again. He pro-

Cartoons like Thomas Nast's "The Cradle of Liberty in Danger" contributed to Ben Butler's failure to win re-election to Congress in 1874. The caption reads, " 'Fee-Fi-Fo-Fum!' The Genie of Massachusetts smells Blue Blood."

claimed martial law, promising "to restore order, maintain public tranquillity and enforce peace and quiet under the laws and constitution of the United States." When the mayor refused to co-operate as Butler wanted, he took over complete civil administration.

It was Butler the military governor that produced his legendary infamy. His image as the scoundrel in uniform, the grafter, looter, thief, murderer, degrader of women, and pilferer of spoons was one the South would never relinquish. But Butler was less a headlong sinner than a victim of bad publicity, albeit self-generated. What he did, typically, was to challenge the gentry, the leaders of the community, by appealing to the artisans and mechanics to make a common cause against the mercantile aristocracy. It was Butler the sans-culotte that the South never forgave.

Butler was still the able administrator. Even his most ardent enemies admitted that the white workers employed by his sanitary commission had cleaned up the city as it had never been cleaned up before. He opened stores, set prices, and established a program of relief for the poor. As for his notorious Woman Order, it was so effective that it never had to be acted upon. Once General Order No. 28 was proclaimed, the tiny Confederate flags vanished from Rebel bosoms; no longer did young ladies dash to the piano to play "The Bonnie Blue Flag" when Yankee officers passed their houses; nor did they do any more spitting.

For poor-relief monies Butler assessed wealthy individuals and corporations, some of whom saw their possessions sold at auction. Relentlessly, skillfully, Butler ferreted out hidden bank assets and recovered funds taken from the United States mint. Southerners who concealed their wealth in European consulates found no lasting protection in foreign flags; Butler did not hesitate to break into the house of a liquor dealer who doubled as the Netherlands consul to seize 800,000 Mexican dollars. He easily persuaded the poor, the Northern-born, and the half-castes to take the oath of allegiance to the Federal government. Officials of the old governing class who refused to take the oath were forced from office. When an obscure gambler named Mumford pulled down the American flag from the roof of the mint and tore it to shreds, Butler, despite protests and threats, hanged him in front of the building. Mumford became a Confederate martyr, as did Mrs. Philip Phillips, who laughed and jeered at a funeral procession for a Yankee lieutenant—and was thrown into military prison on Ship Island.

As military governor, Butler showed a racial attitude more liberal than one might have expected of a Hunker Democrat. He abolished segregated streetcars, put white workers next to colored, and established a "Native Guard" regiment of Negroes as well as two regiments of loyal poor whites. The only segregation he recognized was between Unionists and Secessionists.

In all, Butler did a creditable job of running New Orleans. Yet always, as in Massachusetts, the scent of corruption followed him; there was a sense of chicanery, of underhanded transactions. He maintained that contraband trading with the enemy was necessary in order to obtain supplies; still, the profits in such trade for those around him were enormous. But that Butler himself stole, or made money on official transactions, is not credible. His mills in Massachusetts were bringing in huge profits; his law firm was prospering through his subordinates. He was too well off to have to speculate or peculate. Yet those around him did, and he knew it. Southern heirlooms picked up by Yankee officers for pittances at auctions went north by the carload. Butler's brother Andrew drove a sharp trade in cattle, sugar, cotton, and other Confederate commodities; he was said to have made between $500,000 and $2,000,000 in such enterprises.

European nations objected violently to Butler's cavalier treatment of their New Orleans consulates, and complained to Secretary of State William H. Seward. Finally, in December of 1862, Lincoln removed the controversial general for reasons that were obvious to many, although they were never really spelled out. In his farewell address to the citizens of New Orleans, Butler struck a familiar pose: "I saw that this Rebellion was a war of aristocrats against the middling man, of the rich against the poor; a war of the land-owner against the laborer; the few against the many; and I found no conclusion to it, save in the subjugation of the few and the disenthrallment of the many. I therefore felt no hesitation in taking the substance of the wealthy, who had caused the war, to free the innocent poor, who had suffered by the war."

Butler, the unemployed general, returned North as the hero of the Radicals—indeed, he had moved the full arc from Hunker Democrat to abolitionist Republican. Radicals like Benjamin Wade and Thaddeus Stevens began to see him as a presidential possibility.

It took almost a year for Lincoln to decide what to do with his obstreperous general. Butler was now doubly important politically, both as an old Democrat and as a new Radical. It was necessary, Lincoln saw, to give him some position, if only to keep him out of politics. Late in 1863 Butler was given command of the Department of Virginia and North Carolina.

The following April, the army's newly appointed General in Chief, U. S. Grant, conferred with Butler on Grant's proposed spring offensive against Richmond. Grant was dubious about Butler's military ability and bolstered him with Major Generals Quincy A. Gillmore and William F. "Baldy" Smith. Lincoln was considering burying Butler in the obscurity of the Vice Presidency, but when Simon Cameron relayed the offer of second spot on the Republican ticket for 1864, Butler turned it down: "Tell him . . . I would not quit the field to be Vice President, even with himself as President, unless he will give me bond with sureties, in the full sum of his four years' salary, that he will die or resign within three months after his inauguration." Events were to give the statement a macabre tone: Mr. Lincoln was dead within a few weeks of his inauguration.

In Grant's battle plan, Butler's forces were to form the fourth prong of an attack on Richmond, thrusting from Fortress Monroe up the James River to attack from the rear. Butler's troops occupied Bermuda Hundred, only twelve miles from Richmond, without opposition. Caught off guard, the Confederates had left their capital defended by only a skeleton force. Had he been a daring commander, Butler might have committed his forces at once and taken the city there and then. But, bluffed as to the strength of the defenses, wary before the unknown, and with a civilian's fear of casualties in a bloody frontal attack, he hesitated. And Smith and Gillmore proceeded with a nonprofessional caution that made failure certain. A makeshift Confederate force drove Butler back to the Bermuda Hundred neck. Butler later blamed his subordinates, and even had Gillmore arrested for "mil-

In 1878 Nast's "In the Matrimonial Market Again" portrayed gubernatorial aspirant Butler as a husbandless mother with her fiscal brain-child. "Will Massachusetts accept this Encumbrance?" asks the caption. "No," said the voters.

itary incapacity." To Smith's plea that the amateur general be got rid of, Grant replied sadly that he could not. Butler was still too strong politically.

Butler had one more chance for military triumph. Wilmington, North Carolina, the last port of entry for supplies to the South, lay within his department. If he could seize Fort Fisher, on the promontory that was the key to Wilmington, the city would fall and the Confederacy would face starvation. Butler concocted a scheme for putting the fort out of action by exploding a ship full of gunpowder directly in front of it.

Grant took a dim view of the idea, but he allowed Butler to go ahead and try it. Butler insisted on leading the military-naval expedition himself. When it came, the explosion was so ineffective that the Fort Fisher garrison thought a blockade runner had burst a boiler. Of the 6,500 troops Butler took to capture the fort, only one third landed on shore. Even so, these were enough to have taken the fort—had not Butler again lost his nerve. Alarmed at news that the fort was receiving reinforcements, he ordered a precipitate retreat. Seven hundred of his men were stranded, and had to be rescued by a disgusted Admiral David Porter, who had directed the naval part of the operation. The crew of Porter's flagship manufactured a leather medal for Butler: on one side was a pair of running legs and the stars of a major general; on the other, the legend "In commemoration of his heroic conduct before Fort Fisher, Dec. 1864." On January 8, 1865, Lincoln ordered Butler to "repair to Lowell, Mass."

Hours after Lincoln's assassination, Butler joined in caucus with Radical Republican leaders determined to get rid of "Lincoln influences." Elected to Congress in 1866, Butler became head of the Committee on Reconstruction, and one of the South's most unforgiving opponents. In the coming years his best efforts were directed at impeaching Andrew Johnson, whose conciliatory attitude he regarded as treasonable. The President's removal of Secretary of War Edwin M. Stanton, contrary to the Radical-sponsored Tenure of Office Act that required senatorial consent for such actions, gave Butler and his colleagues the pretext they had been waiting for. Johnson, for his defiance of the Radicals, should be impeached—and Ben Butler would spearhead the proceedings.

All Butler's legal adroitness went into the trial. His grating voice opened the proceedings in a savage four-hour speech to the Senate, sitting as the court of judgment. A *Harper's Weekly* reporter observed him as:

a man whose large pudgy body seemed literally bursting out of his extraordinary swallow tail coat, exposing a broad expanse of not too immaculate linen, and whose massive bald head with its little fringe of oily curls was probably familiar to every occupant of the galleries, for Benjamin F. Butler had not hidden his light under a bushel. There was power in the man's coarse, big-featured face, force and aggressiveness in every line, but his curiously ill-mated eyes with their half-closed lids, his hard mouth and small, drooping moustache, all combined to create an uncomfortable impression of cunning and insincerity, and his whole personality was unattractive.

When the Senate failed by one vote to give the necessary two-thirds majority for conviction, a Washington newspaper put out an extra edition headlined "Suicide of Ben Butler."

But suicide, physical or political, was far from Butler's mind. The postwar era gave him a renewed sense of life. His voice became one of the most feared—and applauded—in the capital. He now made Negro rights and fiat money the cornerstones of his philosophy, whether out of conviction or expediency no one knew. He maneuvered one of the first civil-rights bills through Congress, and fought for the suppression of the Ku Klux Klan. After an Ohio-born carpetbagger had been horsewhipped by night riders in Mississippi, Butler brandished the victim's bloodstained shirt in the House; the phrase "waving the bloody shirt" came to mean appealing to Civil War sentiments for political reasons.

Butler went out of his way to be friendly to the new colored congressmen and to Negroes generally—

so much so that he was hailed at a Negro banquet in New Orleans as a general with a "white face, but a black heart."

Butler and Grant reached something of a détente after Grant reached the White House. The President favorably reappraised Butler's war record, and Butler became one of the administration's chief spokesmen. Yet privately, Butler considered Grant an ignoramus.

Butler took a noisy and active part in setting up carpetbag governments in the South and in supporting them with Northern bayonets. But for all his publicly vengeful attitude toward the South, he could be privately and quietly kind. When the destitute widow of Mumford, the man he had hanged in New Orleans, appealed to him, Butler found her a job.

Conservative Republicans of Massachusetts, their Whig instincts still intact, continued to have little use for Butler. And when he embraced the ultimate State Street heresy of greenback currency, of paying off war debts in depreciated paper, Boston Brahmins persuaded one of their own—Richard Henry Dana, author of *Two Years Before the Mast*—to run as a hard-money Democrat against him in the next congressional election. Butler, sniping away at the "codfish aristocracy," beat Dana six to one.

Forcing his Ku Klux Klan bill through Congress in 1872 was one of Butler's great victories, one that brought him to the height of his national political power. On that crest he attempted to win the nomination for governor, but his entrenched enemies in Massachusetts were able to thwart his ambitions in the Republican conventions of 1872 and 1873. In 1874 they even succeeded in preventing his renomination for Congress, though by waving the bloody shirt he got himself re-elected two years later.

Somehow Butler still found time for his private concerns; he was a much-sought lawyer with a flourishing practice. In a suit over prize money for Confederate ships seized during the war, he won an award of $1,500,000 for Admiral Farragut and his crews—the highest damages sustained up to that time by the Supreme Court. Yet for all his legal eminence, Ben Butler remained the impudent young man who had once tweaked an editor's nose. When a judge asked him testily if he was trying to show contempt for the court, he replied that he was trying to conceal it.

With law and politics came business ventures. In addition to his mills he now owned a granite quarry and the United States Cartridge Company. He speculated in land, in mines, in a barge company. Conflict of interest never troubled him. If he could use his influence to further his enterprises, so much the better. To "Butlerize" was a word coined by his enemies meaning to make off with everything in sight. Butler's activities—and his toadlike bald head and bloated face—became the delight of cartoonist Thomas Nast.

True to his New England heritage, Butler loved the sea. He built a summer home near Gloucester, overlooking Ipswich Bay. He relaxed by sailing his yacht *America,* the famous cup-winner and Confederate blockade-runner. He dressed his crew in snappy uniforms and often participated in the races off Newport, Rhode Island. A spanking nor'wester was an exhilaration: alerted by the Coast Survey when a storm was brewing, he would don his oilskins and put to sea.

In 1878 Butler announced that he was through with both major parties and allowed himself to be nominated by the Greenbackers for the governorship of Massachusetts. But at the same time he was moving back toward the Democratic party of his youth (he even came out for pensions for Confederate veterans); his real goal was to become the Democratic gubernatorial candidate. He arranged for his supporters to pack the convention hall, and he was in fact nominated—to the disgust of the conservative Democrats, who walked out to nominate their own man. The split insured a Republican victory. Conservative Republicans were delighted at Butler's defeat. Mild-mannered President Hayes wrote that it was one of the best events since the war; he considered Butler "unscrupulous, able, rich, untiring, the most dangerous and wicked demagogue we ever had." Butler was an unsuccessful gubernatorial candidate again in 1879, and the following year he refused to run for any office.

Ben's wife, Sarah, had died of cancer in 1876; in 1881 his son Ben-Israel succumbed to Bright's disease. Butler was again nominated for governor by the Democrats and Greenbackers, but in that sad year the candidate's sharp tongue and rasping voice were muted. He scarcely campaigned at all and seemed indifferent to his inevitable defeat.

But by 1882 his spirits were largely recovered, and this time the perennial Democratic gubernatorial nominee had the backing of the likes of Wendell Phillips, Susan B. Anthony, and prison reformer Burnham Wardwell. And, at last, Butler was successful.

In spite of the fair promise of his inaugural address —he said he would reform the criminal code and the state penal institutions, abolish the poll tax, give women the vote, and lower the hours of labor while increasing wages—the new governor was able to do little in the face of a Republican legislature and governor's council. Harvard again became his whipping boy following his "exposure" of the previous administration's selling of paupers' bodies from the Tewksbury almshouse to the Harvard Medical School. "The selling and tanning of human skins," he declared, "was an established industry in Massachusetts!" Breaking

BARNACLE BEN ⚓ THE SAILOR

The yacht *America* was a well-travelled twenty-two-year-old when, in June of 1873, Ben Butler bought her for a mere $5,000. (He was the only bidder at an auction kindly arranged by cronies in the Navy Department. He even had his prize refitted—at government expense—at the Charlestown Navy Yard.) After her smashing victory off the Isle of Wight in 1851, the *America* had gone through several private ownership changes and, temporarily renamed the *Camilla,* had seen duty as a Confederate blockade-runner. The Rebels scuttled her near Jacksonville, Florida, in 1862, but the Federal government raised her for use as a dispatch ship and blockader. For a few years after the war she was a training ship at the United States Naval Academy. Then Butler bought her and, with his smartly uniformed crew, raced and cruised her off the New England coast until his death in 1893, though with declining frequency toward the end. By 1901, her yachting career was over; she lay in neglect until she was presented to the Naval Academy in 1921, but even at Annapolis she continued in disuse. Little more than a rotted hull, she was broken up in 1945. So, although he could not have realized it, Ben Butler had been the *America*'s master during the last of her glory years. In sailing vessels (as, legendarily, in flatware), Butler refused to settle for anything short of the best. —*J.L.P.*

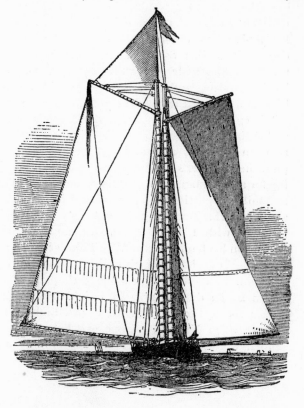

a 250-year tradition, Harvard refused that year to give the governor an honorary doctor's degree. Butler attended the commencement anyhow; so indignant was the president of the alumni association that he resigned in order to avoid receiving him.

In the election of 1883 Butler charged that the Republicans were importing "repeaters" from outside the state to defeat him, and he ordered his 9th Massachusetts Regiment (mostly Irishmen) to guard the polls. He prepared a magnificent display of fireworks on Belvidere's grounds to celebrate his re-election. There was no celebration. Massachusetts voters had tired of his bombast, and Butler was through in state politics.

As he resumed his legal practice, nebulous thoughts of the White House occurred to him; in 1884 he accepted the presidential nomination of the Greenback and Anti-Monopoly parties, hoping that this splinter movement would enhance his chances at the Democratic National Convention, to which he was a delegate-at-large. But the resurgent white South would have nothing to do with Spoons Butler. He could not even find a spokesman to place his name in nomination. After the Democrats nominated Grover Cleveland as their hard-money candidate, Butler toured the country in a gaily painted private railroad car, telling workers that if Cleveland were elected they would starve. When he spoke in Detroit, hecklers tossed tin spoons on the stage, and elsewhere he was jeered as the "Benedict Arnold of American politics." He received a mere 175,000 votes out of ten million, which ended his political career with a humiliating anticlimax.

Butler devoted his remaining years to law, which he said was like chess; and when money and popularity no longer mattered, the game itself was still intriguing. He took many unpopular cases—he defended Chicago's Haymarket Square anarchists, for example—that paid him little or nothing. He grew rheumatic, hard of hearing, and flabby (his daughter Blanche put him on a diet and reduced his weight to 220 pounds).

His enemies and the anti-Butler legends endured, and their target began to grow solicitous of his reputation. In 1892 his thousand-page autobiography was published. *Butler's Book* was an enormous undertaking for an old man, yet the Butler swagger, shrewdness, and military partisanship are stamped in its pages like a watermark. The book interestingly described his relations with Lincoln and Grant, and vindictively carried on his feud with the West Point generals whom he accused of sabotaging his military career. The postwar years he crowded into a single chapter.

Ben Butler died in 1893 while in Washington preparing a case for the Supreme Court. Eight veterans (two of them Negroes, on one of whom Butler had pinned the Congressional Medal of Honor) accompanied his body back to Lowell. He lay in his coffin in the drawing room at Belvidere, a rose in his buttonhole, and, thanks to the undertakers, a smile on his face. He was buried on a bitter-cold January day; a service was held at St. Anne's Episcopal Church, to which he belonged but in whose creed—as he had admitted to Sarah—he had ceased to believe.

The funeral cortege, led by a hearse with six black-plumed horses, extended a mile and a half. All the bells of Lowell tolled as the coffin was drawn across the Merrimack bridge to the cemetery, and the crowds were so great that half a dozen onlookers were injured in the crush. In attendance were state politicians and men of prominence from the governor on down, even to the codfish aristocracy—who kept their fingers crossed against the appearance of any future Ben Butler.

Time has shown Ben Butler to be one of the most arresting political figures that Massachusetts has ever produced; certainly the most caricatured and most vilified; possibly the most astute. "God made me only one way," he once said. "I must always be with the under-dog in the fight. I can't help it; I can't change it, and upon the whole I don't want to." Butler may have Butler-ized, but he also helped the immigrant workers when Know-Nothingism ran high in his state. Whatever his subsequent war record, he rallied the Breckinridge Democrats to the Union at a critical moment. He spoke out for civil rights far in advance of his day. Even his Greenback heresy of managed paper money would become orthodox reality after World War II. Those who thought themselves the better people, both in the North and in the South, despised and distrusted him, and he capitalized on their hate. The workers and the shanty Irish and the Negroes loved him, and not without reason.

Though Belvidere still perches serenely on its hill above the Merrimack, Lowell's textile mills have been gone since the Depression; the grey industrial city has forgotten Butler. Two miles across the river there is a cemetery within a cemetery, a plot surrounded by a locked fence, the grave of an ex-governor and ex-general. There is a headstone of polished granite, but there is no flag to go with it.

Mr. Russell is one of AMERICAN HERITAGE'*s most frequent contributors, his latest article having been "The Harding Papers: . . . and Some Were Saved," in the February, 1965, issue. He expects to publish shortly a biographical study entitled* The Shadow of Blooming Grove: the Hundred Years of Warren G. Harding. *His primary sources for the article above were* Lincoln's Scapegoat General, *by Richard S. West, Jr. (Houghton, 1965),* Stormy Ben Butler, *by Robert S. Holzman (Macmillan, 1954), and, of course,* Butler's Book.

Grass

CONTINUED FROM PAGE 32

BIG BLUESTEM

lowed the buffalo. The tribes themselves—Blackfoot, Crow, Cheyenne, Pawnee, Arapaho, Apache, Comanche—had an ideal relationship with their environment: the Indian lived off the buffalo; the buffalo lived off the grass. Colonel Richard Irving Dodge reported seeing a herd of buffalo numbering over 500,000. The grass could sustain herds that big without danger of being overgrazed, for by instinct the buffalo moved with the seasonal growth of the grass.

Sometimes, to make their hunting easier, the Indians burned the grass, but the homesteaders, who began to come in 1862, were the first to break the sod. They had to, first to make their sod houses and then to cultivate their 160 acres. Pioneers came in great numbers from the East, from Europe, even from Australia, encouraged by Congress and the railroads. A small registration fee and a five-year occupancy were all Congress required before giving away the land. And the homesteaders plowed away.

The first sight of the tall grasses waving over an expanse of rolling land often inspired the newcomers with a kind of "seasickness," or fear, or exhilaration, or loneliness. In 1837, Buckingham had noted: "I never felt so strongly the sense of loneliness as here."

For the homesteaders it was the same. Beret Hansa, in O. E. Rölvaag's *Giants in the Earth*, exclaimed: "Why there isn't even a thing that one can *hide behind!*" From the door of her sod house the plainswoman looked out on grass whispering in the wind, scorched by the sun, and if she dared go out herself she would get lost. Or the wind would turn her face to leather, as it was turning her man to leather as he plowed up the land around the sod house. The walls of that house were held together by the roots of the grass, and the mud floor was strewn with grass. Sometimes, twisted into hanks and tossed into the stove, the grass even heated the house. The homesteader's wife worried about water; soon the windmill would bring her water from deep below the topsoil. But what would bring water to the soil?

This was in the eighteen sixties. In 1873, the settlers were hit with the first bad drought. In 1874, the locusts came, Rocky Mountain grasshoppers which ate the leaves and stems of the grasses—and not only every green thing but even the clothes off the line. The settlers panicked; some left, convinced that it would take a special kind of human being to stick it out here in an environment they themselves knew nothing about.

Meanwhile, in southwest Texas, longhorn cattle, originally raised on the old Spanish missions, now roamed wild. The North, hungry after the Civil War, was screaming for beef. Northward cattle drives had begun as early as the mid-1830's, but those herds were small compared with these that were now beginning. As the buffalo was killed off (and the Indian with him, practically), the longhorns, the cowboys, and the cattle ranchers took over as much open range in the Plains as they could manage. But unlike the buffalo, the longhorns did not move with the seasonal growth of the grasses. They were either fenced in by the ranchers near water, or fenced out by homesteaders protecting their farms. Overcrowding of the range began. Ranchers, finding the grass cheap fodder, let their longhorns graze all year round, and fought for water rights with the homesteaders—who now, under the Desert Land Act of 1877, could have an entire section, 640 acres, provided only that they would irrigate it. (The irrigation provision, alas, was often met by throwing a bucket of water on the grass.)

By the mid-1880's, cattle ranches had spread north into the short-grass country, into Colorado, Wyoming, and Montana. In his pioneering survey of the Plains presented to Congress in 1878, John Wesley Powell had pointed out that this vast area of public domain was not being properly used. In an arid and sub-humid climate most of the soil does not contain enough moisture to permit farming by the usual methods. Most of the region, Powell felt, was not suitable for farming at all; grazing was its best use. But not the kind that was then going on: letting the cattle graze all through spring, summer, autumn, and winter, never giving the grass a chance to renew itself. Powell recommended that pasture lands be parcelled out in lots of 2,560 acres and held in common, with all the participating ranchers responsible for the right use of them.

But western politicians in Congress, land speculators, and cattlemen, all of them in a hurry to profit from the bounty of the region, could not halt for planning. Cattle grazing was causing more injury to the land than farming, Powell said. And then there were the sheep. Both the farmer and the rancher turned on the sheepman; they said his animals' thin muzzles and sharp teeth cropped the grass to the ground, while their spiky hoofs pockmarked the soil.

All—homesteader, rancher, sheep farmer—were busy destroying the grass.

Then, in the eighteen nineties, the sod was really stripped away as huge wheat farms were established in the Red River valley in Minnesota and North Dakota—farms sometimes as large as 65,000 acres.

Drought struck in the 1890's, and again in 1900, in 1910, and in 1917. But the World War I years were good for the wheat farmer, and he survived. By 1924, in spite of the dry spells, Plains farmers were growing seventeen million more acres of wheat than they had grown in 1909. Arid, short-grass regions of Oklahoma, Texas, New Mexico, Wyoming, and Montana, where plow should never have furrowed a sod, were being farmed.

The day of reckoning had to come.

The story of the Dust Bowl is well known. There had been dust storms in the Plains before, but never anything like those that began to darken the sky in the early nineteen thirties. Black clouds of prairie soil were blown as far eastward as Washington, D.C. And farther: the dust was visible two hundred miles at sea.

The grass was gone, and there was nothing to prevent the dust from blowing. Farmers and cowboys, trying to work in dust, got only failed crops, thin and dying cattle, and mounting debts. Nearly four and a half million people lived in the Plains in the early nineteen thirties before the drought; within five years, forty thousand families moved out, leaving vast areas of the land not only denuded but uninhabited.

Finally, where individuals had failed, Washington took a hand. With the Bankhead-Jones Act of 1937, the federal government reacquired some of the lands that had been vacated, and made loans to farmers who stayed on, to begin soil conservation measures.

Biologists like F. W. Albertson and ecologists like J. E. Weaver now began to help in the study of what had been ignored, for the most part, all along: the grasses themselves. Many of the recommendations in the Great Plains report of 1936 were aimed at one end: restoring the grasses. But that was a big job: nature had taken ages to put them there. Scientists—and the Department of Agriculture, with its Soil Conservation Service and Forest Service—set to work. First, surveys were made. Next, the government acquired large areas of range and granted use of them, under rules of controlled grazing, to permittees. Water resources were developed through a series of dams and irrigation projects. Finally, Washington sought the co-operation of local governments and private owners in projects to control erosion and promote proper grazing.

The program put into motion by the government—and by the private agencies and individual landowners whose co-operation it enlisted—had three objectives: converting essentially nonarable cropland back to range or natural grassland; re-establishing the native grasses on depleted and killed-out range areas or on worked-out farm land that had simply been allowed to go back to whatever vegetation developed; and encouraging the people of the region to adopt improved methods of land management.

For the conversion and re-establishment processes the first requirement, of course, was a supply of seeds. In special Plant Materials Centers set up by the Soil Conservation Service throughout the Great Plains, various strains of native grasses—such as the gramas, bluestems, switchgrass, and indiangrass—were produced. The process was far from simple: strains of little bluestem which thrived in Texas, for example, might not survive in the Dakotas. The Agriculture Department's Agricultural Research Service, notably the center under the direction of Dr. L. C. Newell at the University of Nebraska, made a major contribution in discovering which grasses would grow best in various Plains areas. Then, special machines were developed to plant the seed.

Finally, farmers were encouraged to stop plowing land that was not meant to be plowed, and to put it to its proper use: grazing. The Soil Conservation Service also suggested to them—and to ranchers as well—how the land ought to be grazed: rotationally, with grazing deferred on some grasses until early summer so that they could get a good spring start. Typically, a conservation plan for an entire farm or ranch would be developed, with the government sharing the costs of re-establishing the grasses.

The recovery of the Great Plains and the bringing back of the grass were not accomplished by human measures alone. Nature herself helped out. Beginning in 1941 with the coming of wet years again, the land itself began to go through its almost miraculous, age-old cycle. Weaver and Albertson observed and documented this recovery of the native grasses: first the primeval weeds came back—goosefoot, tumbleweed, and common sunflower; then a second weed stage began—little barley, peppergrass, and stickseeds; thereafter, early native grasses began to return—sand dropseed, western wheat grass, false buffalo grass; finally, the mature native grasses—the gramas, buffalo grass, three-awns—were seen again.

Today, driving through the Great Plains region, the traveller will often pass signs bearing the initials

BLUE GRAMA

"U.S.," with a bunch of grass between the "U." and the "S." This sign indicates he is travelling through National Grasslands. On June 20, 1960, nearly four million acres of federal lands were so designated. They are managed by the Forest Service and are set up as outdoor recreational areas, range land, wildlife habitats, and fishing preserves. These lands are public domain. Artificial lakes have been created for water sports and for conservation purposes; thirty campsites now dot the Plains and more are being prepared; hunters flock to the Dakotas each year for the ringneck pheasant, to Wyoming and Montana for geese, duck, and Barbary sheep. There are over three million acres of unposted land to which we have free access, and it is all covered with grass. The names of the new grasslands are old and familiar: the Comanche in Colorado, the Cimarron in southwest Kansas, the Pawnee in northeastern Colorado, the Oglala in Nebraska, the Kiowa in New Mexico.

But the National Grasslands are only the most visible results of what will go down in history as one of

BUFFALO GRASS

the major conservation efforts of modern times. Thanks to the cropland-conversion, range-reseeding, and land-management programs, the grasslands of the ten Great Plains states are in better condition today than they have been for seventy-five years. The environment has come full cycle: once more a rich carpet of grass holds the Plains in place, letting the land fulfill itself—and the men who live on it and draw their sustenance from it.

Mr. Murray teaches creative writing at the University of Iowa and farms five acres at nearby West Branch. Mr. Wilson, a free-lance photographer with a special interest in conservation, lives on Bainbridge Island, Washington. He took many of the photos in this portfolio for his Grass Land, *published by Wide Skies Press in Polk, Nebraska.*

The "Military Crimes" of Charles Lee CONTINUED FROM PAGE 15

hear. Nor did he understand the full significance of Greene's comment about the people's expectations. Throughout the winter at Valley Forge, Washington and his supporters had fought off an attempt to replace him as Commander in Chief with Horatio Gates, the hero of Saratoga. This so-called Conway Cabal—named after one of the chief schemers, the Irish-French general Thomas Conway—was in retrospect a pitifully fumbling affair, a battle of pygmies against a giant. But Washington and the men around him took it very seriously.

Washington soon demonstrated his own inclination by sending the stipulated 1,500 men under Brigadier General Charles Scott to worry Clinton's left flank and by detaching Daniel Morgan with 600 riflemen to harass the right. The next day he added 1,000 men under Anthony Wayne and told them to link up with Brigadier General William Maxwell's New Jersey brigade of 1,300 men, supported by some 800 militia, who were already hanging on the British rear. To co-ordinate these detachments, he placed Lafayette, wholehearted supporter of an attack, in command.

At first Charles Lee agreed to let Lafayette take charge. The job, he said, called for "a young volunteering general." But when he saw that the force amounted to some 5,000 men, he changed his mind. It would, he told Washington, "have an odd appearance" if he as senior major general permitted one of

his juniors to take command of what amounted to almost half the American army. With considerable reluctance, Washington agreed to the change.

On the morning of June 27 Lee took charge of the American advance forces. By now it was clear that the British were marching to embark at Sandy Hook, taking the shortest possible land route across New Jersey. In another day—or two at the most—they would be beyond reach. Clinton had divided his 11,000-man force into three main divisions: 5,000 moving at the head of the supply train; behind it, 4,000 under Clinton's immediate command; and a rear guard of 2,000 elite foot soldiers and cavalry under Lord Cornwallis. On June 27, the British camped around the straggling village of Monmouth Court House. On June 28, at 4 A.M., the advance guard and baggage train resumed the march.

The sun rose that morning with a promise of ferocity in its glow. By 10 A.M., when Lee moved out with his men to deliver his "partial stroke," the sandy countryside, dotted with patches of scrub pine and cut by deep ravines, was a ninety-six-degree oven.

The events of the next few hours resulted in a soon-famous encounter on the field between Washington and Charles Lee, and in Lee's court-martial for disobedience and for a "disorderly and shameful retreat." The story emerges dramatically from the testimony of the witnesses who began taking the stand on that not-yet-certified Independence Day of 1778.

The Judge Advocate General was twenty-eight-year-old John Laurance, a well-trained New York lawyer and son-in-law of Lee's old friend Alexander McDougall. Under the Articles of War, Laurance was responsible for questioning both prosecution and defense witnesses. The defendant also had the right to cross-examine freely, and it soon became clear that Lee would exercise that right strenuously.

First came Brigadier Generals Charles Scott and Anthony Wayne. Scott was a tough, stocky Virginian who had fought as a noncommissioned officer with Washington on the ill-fated Braddock expedition and had distinguished himself at Trenton and Brandywine Creek. He had also headed the list of nine brigadiers who had protested to Congress the promotion of Thomas Conway to major general at the height of the intrigue. Wayne, whose courage in attack would earn him the nickname Mad Anthony, was equally tough and aggressive. Two days after the battle they had written a joint letter to Washington accusing Lee of retreating without warning and leaving them in a perilous position. Their letter had played no small part in bringing on the court-martial.

Scott told of asking Lee for orders as they began the march: "General Lee said he had none." Cross-examining, Lee asked Scott if Washington's orders meant that they were to attack the enemy regardless of whether the British were a slight covering party "or whether the greater part of the flower of their troops, as it turned out?" Scott stubbornly insisted, "I understood we were to have attacked the enemy at all events."

When Wayne testified, Lee asked him the same question and got the same answer. In reply to another question, Wayne went even further than Scott, bluntly declaring that from Washington's conversation with Lee before the battle it was clear—to Wayne at least—that the Commander in Chief was ready to bring on a general action.

Next came the testimony of Washington's aides. Lieutenant Colonel Richard K. Meade told how on the morning of June 28 Washington had sent him with a verbal message to Lee ordering him to put his troops in motion, leaving his packs behind, and to bring on an attack as soon as possible. Meade said that Lee had complained bitterly of conflicting intelligence and had protested that he already had sent one unit forward in obedience to an earlier Washington command, and he considered it to be in grave danger. Cross-examining, Lee asked Meade if he thought Washington had wanted to bring on a general action. Meade's reply was unwaveringly affirmative.

A man now testified who, Lee sensed, was one of his genuine enemies: brash, twenty-three-year-old Alexander Hamilton. He instinctively disliked Lee and had no sympathy whatsoever for his ideas about a people's war. Immediately after the battle, Hamilton had written to Congressman Elias Boudinot of New Jersey that "the finest opportunity America ever possessed [has] been fooled away by a man in whom she has placed a large share of the most ill-judged confidence ... I mean General Lee. This man is either a driveler in the business of soldiership or something much worse."

Hamilton backed up Scott, Wayne, and Meade, declaring his conviction that "General Washington's intention was fully to have the enemy attacked on their march, and that the circumstances must be very extraordinary and unforeseen, which, consistent with his wish, could justify the not doing it."

"Did you, either by letter to me, or in conversation with me, communicate this idea of General Washington's intention as fully and clearly as you have done it to the Court?" Lee asked.

"I do not recollect that I ever did," Hamilton admitted.

Next came the Marquis de Lafayette, about Hamilton's age, wearing the epaulets of a major general. The boyish, sandy-haired French nobleman had been in the United States for thirteen months by this time and had acquired fluent English and a son's adoration for George Washington. He too had played a leading role in defeating the Conway Cabal, but unlike Hamilton, he did not see Lee as a similar threat to Washington's authority. His testimony was reluctant and more than a little vague. He described having marched out with Lee that morning "as a volunteer." Under orders from a Lee aide, he led part of the American column in an attempt to strike the British left flank. Some of his troops having come under fire of British artillery, he began organizing them to charge the battery; then he looked behind him and saw the rest of Lee's force retreating. So instead of attacking, he fell back too and found Lee near Monmouth village, ordering "that the troops should take post farther back." No sooner had they formed than Lee was told that the enemy was attacking *his* left flank, and he ordered another retreat. "While this was doing," Lafayette testified, "General Washington arrived."

Judge Advocate Laurance now asked Lafayette a blunt question. "Did the troops under the command of General Lee, to your knowledge, make any attack on the enemy the 28th of June?"

"I cannot say that I saw them make any attack on the enemy," Lafayette replied.

Lee promptly asked: "If any attack had been made ... were you in a position [to] have seen it?"

"No," Lafayette admitted. He also admitted that

early in the day, as they maneuvered to cut off what they hoped was the enemy rear guard, Lee had said: "My dear Marquis, I think those people are ours."

Lee then asked him a question that he was to repeat again and again. "Did you observe in my voice, manner, appearance, air or countenance, that I was in the least disconcerted, or whether, on the contrary, I was not tranquil and cheerful?"

"It seemed to me by your voice and features," Lafayette said, somewhat ambiguously, "you were then as you are in general."

In response to questions by the court, Lafayette said he had seen no sign of Lee having "any general compact plan" and said that "the orders for retreating came from General Lee," adding that "there was a great confusion and contrariety in the orders, and a complaint amongst the troops on account of it." Finally, perhaps most important, "the number of the enemy did not appear to be equal to ours." Yet Lafayette admitted, "I thought that intelligence had been received that all the British army were coming upon us."

Two days of further testimony threw little more light on the events of June 28, and on July 6 the court adjourned while the army marched toward the Hudson. In the meantime Lee did not help his cause by sending to the New Jersey *Gazette* an open letter in which he spoke bitterly of the "atrocious attack" being made upon his conduct and went on to describe the dubious action at Monmouth as "a very handsome check" to the British, achieved by a "retrograde manoeuvre of near four miles . . . fighting in a variety of places—in the plain and in the woods—by advancing and retreating, the enemy were at last fairly worn down." Anthony Wayne, writing to a friend a few days later, said that this letter "savors of insanity or flows from worse sources."

On July 13, with the court now sitting in Paramus, New Jersey, Lieutenant Colonel John Laurens was sworn. A son of Henry Laurens, the president of the Continental Congress, this darkly handsome young aide was, like his father, totally devoted to George Washington. He told of having delivered a letter from Washington to Lee on June 28 promising the support of the entire army in the ensuing action. Lee, Laurens said, had read the letter, hesitated, confessed he did not really know what to say, and continued his retreat. Laurens thought that "General Lee seemed to be a good deal embarrassed and that his orders [to his subordinates] were indistinct."

"Were you ever in an action before?" asked Lee, no doubt in his most condescending manner.

"I have been in several actions," Laurens snapped. "I did not call that an action, as there was no action previous to the retreat!"

Laurens was followed by Alexander Hamilton, who told how he had gone forward on Washington's orders to reconnoiter the country between the main army and Lee's detachment. He met Lee and his men in full retreat, "issuing out of a wood . . . in two or three small columns. . . ." He said the men "were in themselves in tolerable good order, but seemed to be marching without system or design, as chance should direct." Lee gave his orders, Hamilton said in answer to a question from the Judge Advocate, "under a hurry of mind."

Obviously irked, Lee barked, "Did you not express in the field an idea diametrically reverse of my state of mind?"

In reply, Hamilton gave a hint of the talent for elegant circumlocution that later advanced his career as a lawyer:

I said something to you in the field expressive of an opinion that there appeared in you no want of that degree of self-possession, which proceeds from a want of personal intrepidity. I had no idea in my present evidence of insinuating the most distant charge of this nature, but only to designate that there appeared a certain hurry of spirits which may proceed from a temper not so calm and steady as is necessary to support a man in such critical circumstances.

Several of Washington's other aides then confirmed that Lee had appeared to be in a confused state of mind at Monmouth and that his troops behaved in corresponding fashion. One told of asking Lieutenant Colonel William Smith, John Adams' son-in-law, why they were retreating. Smith said he had no idea; "that they had lost but one man."

Next two more of Washington's aides, James Mc-

Henry and Tench Tilghman, described Washington's confrontation with Lee. Tilghman told how they were leading the main army down the road from English-town, worried because they had had no word from Lee, when a fifer told them that the Americans were in full retreat. Washington became so angry that he ordered the boy put under guard. But the news was soon confirmed when they encountered two stumbling, half-exhausted regiments, worn out not by fighting but by running in the ferocious heat. Moments later Lee himself arrived with his panting column behind him. "General Washington rode up to him with some degree of astonishment, and asked him what was the meaning of this," Tilghman testified.

General Lee answered . . . "Sir, Sir?" I took it that General Lee did not hear the question distinctly.

Upon General Washington's repeating the question, General Lee answered, that from a variety of contradictory intelligence, and that from his orders not being obeyed, matters were thrown into confusion, and that he did not chuse to beard the British army with troops in such a situation. He said that besides, the thing was against his own opinion.

General Washington answered, whatever his opinion might have been, he expected his orders would have been obeyed, and then rode on toward the rear of the retreating troops.

The upshot, as everyone at the trial knew, was that Washington had successfully rallied the retreating Americans, who—under his leadership—had made a skillful and determined stand against several British assaults and had ended the Battle of Monmouth in a draw.

Among several minor prosecution witnesses who followed Tilghman, the most damaging to Lee was Brigadier General William "Scotch Willie" Maxwell, who testified that Lee did not even know on which wing his brigade was posted. Baron von Steuben, no friend of Lee's guerrilla ideas, said he had seen "great disorder." The French volunteer officer Pierre Charles L'Enfant, future architect of the nation's capitol, said that Lee had told him he had "orders from Congress and the General-in-Chief not to engage." On cross-examination, Lee asked L'Enfant if he thought that meant he intended "not to engage at all, or not to engage but in a particular manner."

"I understood that you intended not to engage at all," L'Enfant answered. He said that on the attack of a mere two hundred British, Lee had ordered a general retreat.

The Judge Advocate General now placed in the record two letters Lee had written to Washington as evidence to support the third charge—of "disrespect to the Commander-in-Chief." These underscore one of the principal ironies of the case. Apparently Washington had had no intention of court-martialling Lee. But after sulking for a day, Lee had fired off a long letter declaring that Washington's "singular expressions" on the battlefield had implied that Lee "was guilty either of disobedience of orders, of want of conduct, or want of courage." He demanded to know "on which of these three articles you ground your charge, that I may prepare for my justification . . . to the army, to the Congress, to America, and to the world in general." Although he insisted he had "the greatest respect and veneration for General Washington," Lee was convinced that "some of those dirty earwigs who will forever insinuate themselves near persons in high office" had poisoned Washington's mind against him.

Washington had replied with a very cutting letter, denying that he had used any "singular expressions" and listing the charges against Lee in savagely formal terms. Lee had blazed back a reply, vowing that he was looking forward to the "opportunity of shewing to America the sufficiency of her respective servants" and warning the Commander in Chief not to let "the tinsel dignity" of office "offiscate the bright rays of truth."

By now the army and the court-martial board had crossed the Hudson and were meeting in Peekskill, New York. On July 19, Lee launched his counter-attack by summoning to the stand his aide John Francis Mercer. A headstrong, extremely positive young Virginian, later a foe of the Constitution, Mercer was wholeheartedly dedicated to Lee. According to him, Scott and Wayne had retreated without orders, thereby unhinging Lee's entire battle plan. "Did I not express a great deal of indignation when you

informed me that all the troops [Wayne's men] had left the woods?" Lee asked.

"You did."

In response to another Lee question, Mercer painted a most uncomplimentary picture of Alexander Hamilton's state of mind. He told how Hamilton, after Washington had exchanged severe words with Lee, had ridden up and cried: "I will stay here with you, my dear General, and die with you; let us all die here rather than retreat." Lee, Mercer said, "answered him very coolly, to observe you [Lee] well, to see whether you were discomposed. . . . Colonel Hamilton made answer that he thought you possessed of yourself to a very high degree." Mercer himself pronounced Lee "exceedingly composed." After describing how he had ridden up and down the entire battlefield, he avowed, "I did not see any troops that were in disorder in the course of the day. . . . All the troops that I saw were in perfect good order, as far as the heat of the weather would permit."

Mercer's testimony indicated the general pattern of the trial: just as Washington's aides had uniformly tried to discredit Lee, Lee's aides would uniformly contradict them. One novelty, however, was a deposition from a civilian, Mr. Peter Wikoff, who was "perfectly acquainted with that part of the country where the action had happened on the 28th of June last." Wikoff told how Lee "begged me to conduct his troops under cover of some wood, for he could not make them stand in a plain or open field so well as in the woods. . . . I then pointed out to him a wood and eminence adjoining, which General Lee approved of, and begged me to lead his troops on and shew them the place which I did. The eminence was the very piece of ground His Excellency General Washington afterwards formed his army on."

The court now adjourned to give Lee a chance to prepare his summation. He wrote it out and spent several days polishing it. This was probably a mistake: the final tone was much too literary to move a group of tough soldiers.

Lee began by insisting that the verbal order he had received from Colonel Meade on June 28 had been discretionary. He recalled it as: "The General [Washington] expects you will find means of engaging the enemy, if no powerful consideration prevent you." Lee put special stress on his battlefield discovery of "the great ravine" that cut across the entire plain before Monmouth Court House and had only a single bridge across it. It was the sort of terrain, he said, that might have proved fatal to the Americans had it not been taken into consideration. Compounding this problem, Lee maintained, was the barrage of contradictory intelligence he had received after beginning his advance. Some scouts told him the enemy had marched, others that they had not moved a step from Monmouth Court House. He then narrated how his plan to nip off the British rear guard between the Wayne and Lafayette columns was wrecked by the swift British shift to the offensive.

Thereafter, as Lee saw it, it was simply a question of where to make a stand. Thanks to Wikoff, he had found the right place behind the great ravine and had, he asserted, practically disposed for battle all the troops under his command when Washington rode up. He swore it had never been his intention to make "a general retreat." He had simply fallen back to the best position he could find.

"So far at this time from conceiving ourselves as beaten or disgrac'd . . . I really thought," Lee said, "taking into consideration all circumstances, the various contradictory and false intelligence, disobedience or mistakes in some officers, precipitancy in others, ignorance of the ground, want of cavalry — that it was the flower of the British army we had to deal with . . . I really thought the troops entitled to the highest honor; and that I myself, instead of thundering charges brought against me, had merited some degree of applause from the General and the Public." It was not so much Washington's censorious words that insulted him, Lee explained, but "the manner in which he expressed them [which] was much stronger and more severe than the expressions themselves."

Examining various aspects of the prosecution's evidence, Lee struck hard at Wayne. "I do not mean to deprecate the value of General Wayne (I believe him to be a most thoroughly brave man) but I cannot help observing, that from the moment he took command of

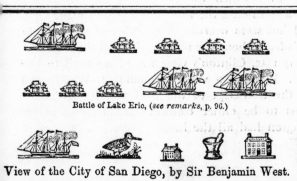

the advanced corps he seem'd to think the whole executive duties of the day transferr'd to him, and that he had nothing to do but make demands for any number of troops he thought proper to dispose of." As for the court's tendency to stress the numbers of the enemy, Lee protested that "as every General makes it his business to conceal his forces [as] much as possible, the visible part of the opponent army is often the least." He said he had originally estimated that the British numbered 2,000 but that it had soon become apparent that "their whole army, or at least their whole flying army" was in the field.

Lee now returned to the point that seemed to annoy him more than anything else—Hamilton's assertion that Lee had been a victim of "hurry of spirits." He reiterated what his aide had already suggested, that it was Hamilton who had been "much flustered and in a sort of frenzy of valour." How was it, Lee asked, that only Hamilton and Laurens had seen agitation when "every other gentleman who had an opportunity of observing me that day" had seen the contrary?

Finally, Lee attempted to dispose of the third charge, disrespect. He asked every member of the court "to substitute himself for a moment in my place, and then to ask his own breast, if instead of the congratulation and applause he had expected, he had been received with slight and reproach, he does not think it possible to write a letter in such or stronger terms than mine, without being actuated by an unruly and contumacious spirit?" Lee avowed his love and respect for "His Excellency." But when Washington's reply brought "thundering charges . . . against me, comprehending the blackest military crimes of the whole black catalogue, I was more than confounded, I was thrown into a stupor. . . ."

The black-and-white pattern of the testimony made it clear to the members of the board that they were being forced to choose between Lee and Washington. The specter of "faction," which had scarcely been exorcised by the defeat of the Conway Cabal, was again haunting the army. They debated for three days, considering "the defendant's will and intent as well as his acts" according to military law. On August 12, the board sonorously announced its verdict. Lee was guilty on all counts, but the word "shameful" was

---

Mr. Fleming, the well-known author of our Verdicts of History series, relied heavily on the Lee Papers, published by the New-York Historical Society in 1872, in preparing the present article; he also consulted at some length with Dr. Francis S. Ronalds, a member of our Advisory Board and an expert on the Revolution. Among published secondary works, the author recommends General Charles Lee: Traitor or Patriot?, *by J. R. Alden (Louisiana State University, 1951).*

deleted from the second charge, which was altered to read, "Guilty of . . . making an unnecessary, and in some few instances a disorderly retreat." The penalty more than anything else revealed the court's sense of embarrassment over the whole affair. Lee was suspended from the army for one year. This was practically an admission of the political nature of the verdict. If the court had really taken seriously its verdict of guilty on the first two charges, the appropriate penalty would have been death before a firing squad.

Is it possible, in the light of history, to reach a more objective verdict? As in most attempts to court-martial an officer for conduct on the field in the midst of a war, there were crucial missing witnesses—the men who had fought on the other side, particularly the enemy Commander in Chief. Except for an official summary report, no British statements on Monmouth appeared for almost 150 years. Then, in 1925, certain papers of Sir Henry Clinton became available, including a careful analysis of that battle.

Clinton completely substantiates Lee's claim that the "whole flying army" was in the field. Hearing "from Lord Cornwallis . . . that the enemy began to appear in force . . . I caused the whole rear guard to face about and return back," Clinton wrote. Quickly divining Lee's flanking scheme, Clinton "came immediately to the resolution of pressing the enemy's advance guard so hard as to oblige the officer commanding it to call back his detachments from my flanks to its assistance." This soon worked, and then, seeing Lee with his back to the great ravine, Clinton decided to risk a general engagement and threw in everything he had, hoping to crush the American detachment before Washington came up. Even if the main army arrived, Clinton reasoned, "Had Washington been blockhead enough to sustain Lee, I should have catched him between two defiles."

In Clinton's opinion, retreat had been Lee's only hope. His "whole corps would probably have fallen into the power of the King's army if he had made a stand in front of the first defile, and not retreated with the precipitancy he did." But the Britisher wrote, of course, out of an unshakable conviction of the total superiority of his regulars over the Americans—a prejudice that Lee unfortunately shared. The skill and ferocity with which the Americans fought off the British attacks once the two armies joined make Clinton's claims seem overconfident and cast some doubt on Lee's fears about the unfavorable terrain.

At any rate, Clinton's view was of no avail to Lee in 1778. Without a word of comment, Washington passed the transcript of the trial and its verdict to Congress to be either confirmed or rejected. Here Washington had all the heavy artillery. Even before the trial began, John Laurens had written several letters to his father, the president of Congress, accusing Lee not only of misconduct but of disloyalty. By the time Lee's aide Evan Edwards reached Philadelphia, intending to urge congressmen to his commander's support, the current of public opinion was running so strongly against Lee that the mortified Edwards wrote to him: "Matters have been so cursedly represented in this place that I have been almost mobb'd in defending you—ten thousand infamous lyes have been spread that I never heard before to byass the minds of the people against you."

When Congress dallied through the fall without coming to a decision, Lee took his case to the newspapers once more. On December 3, the Pennsylvania *Packet* published a three-column blast from Lee's pen insisting that the military court had made no effort to find out just what orders Washington had given him before Monmouth. He lauded American troops but carefully mentioned only victories won by them under commanders other than Washington. He then mentioned a number of resounding Washington defeats and wondered how they could be explained, granted the bravery and ability of the lower American ranks.

Two days later, Congress voted two to one to confirm the verdict of the court-martial. When he heard the news, Lee (according to one story) looked at his favorite dog, Mr. Spada, and cried: "Oh, that I was that animal that I might not call man my brother." Earlier he had written to another anti-Washington officer, Aaron Burr, announcing that he was going to retire to Virginia "and learn to hoe tobacco, which I find is the best school to form a consummate general."

But Lee stayed on in Philadelphia for a while, doing his utmost to make trouble. He urged his friend Gates to resign before Washington's partisans devoured him too; he badgered Congress for money to salvage his debt-encumbered Virginia properties. He fought a paper duel with Baron von Steuben over the German's testimony in the trial and a real duel with John Laurens, who had decided that Lee's reflections on Washington's character called for vengeance. With Hamilton as a second on one side and Evan Edwards backing Lee, the two men blazed away at each other on the edge of a wood near Philadelphia; Lee received a superficial wound in the stomach.

Finally, totally frustrated and almost bankrupt, Lee drifted back to Virginia, where he lived in the crudest poverty on his undeveloped estate, Prato Rio. He continued to stir up trouble wherever he found a willing partner. On June 7 he sent to William Goddard, printer of the Maryland *Journal* and the Baltimore *Advertiser*, a set of "whacking queries"—twenty-five so-called questions, almost all of them assaults on Washington. Goddard printed them anonymously on July 6; two days later, an angry mob forced him to reveal that Lee was the author of the attack and to promise an apology for having slandered Washington.

This was Lee's next-to-last gasp. At the end of his year's suspension from the army, Congressman James Forbes of Maryland offered a resolution "that Major General Charles Lee be informed that Congress have no further occasion for his services in the Army of the United States of America." The resolution was voted down by a narrow margin. Lee's reaction was true to form. In a fury he dashed off a letter: "Congress must know little of me if they suppose that I would accept of their money since the confirmation of the wicked and infamous sentence which was passed upon me." The resolution for Lee's dismissal was then reintroduced, and this time it carried.

Thus ended Charles Lee's connection with the American Revolution. He died in 1782 on a trip to Philadelphia, still bitterly convinced that Washington and his idolaters had deliberately destroyed him. There is just enough truth in the idea to make more than a few historians sympathetic to Charles Lee. On the testimony of the court-martial, the honest verdict probably should have been a hung jury.

But another verdict of history that Lee would have found just as galling is certainly clear from the trial. In spite of all his ostentatious talk and military scholarship, Charles Lee was not a great general. His total failure at Monmouth to reconnoiter the terrain; his indecision and hesitation, which allowed Clinton to outmaneuver him; his failure to inspire either confidence or co-operation in his subordinates—all these mark him as a third-rate leader of men. At Monmouth, George Washington was not only the commanding general, he was the real leader of the American Revolution. The men around him knew it. But Charles Lee chose to learn it the hard way.

A sharp impression of Lee by a contemporary British artist

high priority. The tendency was to stall Disney and to look at his product, if at all, only after screening more commercially promising projects. Disney recalled peeping out through projection-booth windows on the rare occasions when his work was given a showing, trying to gauge the viewers' reactions.

At one of these screenings, a character who was even more legendary than Powers happened to be present, and it was he who sensed the possible exploitation value of Disney's film. His name was Harry Reichenbach, and, as a press agent, he had previously promoted an utterly ordinary piece of kitsch called *September Morn* into a scandal of international proportions. At this time he was managing the Colony Theatre in New York, and he asked permission to book *Steamboat Willie* as an added attraction. Disney was hesitant, fearing that with the New York cream skimmed off, he would have an even more difficult time persuading a national distributor to take the film. Reichenbach argued, however, that this was a special film demanding special treatment. He offered Disney a two-week run beginning September 19, 1928, and Disney talked him into paying $500 a week for the privilege.

The strategy worked. Reichenbach got the press to attend and to write stories about his added attraction, and Disney spent a good deal of time at the Colony listening to the laughter of audiences responding to the first genuinely artistic use of sound film. After the run at the Colony, *Willie* moved to S. L. Rothafel's two-year-old Roxy Theatre. Now the distributors started coming to Disney, asking him what he wanted to do and what they could do to help him. They got only part of the answer they were hoping for: yes, he did want to go on making Mickey Mouse cartoons; no, he did not want to sell them the films outright. In fact, he insisted on retaining complete control of his product. Again it appeared that he had reached an impasse.

It was Pat Powers who rescued him. He was looking for markets and promotion for his Cinephone device. More important, he sensed in the mouse a highly profitable item to distribute. In return for ten per cent of the gross, Powers offered to distribute the Mickey Mouse films through the system of independent, or "state's-rights," bookers. This was one of the simplest and oldest methods of film distribution.

The system had several disadvantages. The most obvious was that it took three sizable slices off the top of the gross—one each for the theatre owner, the state's-rights man, and the national distributor—before any profit dribbled back to the original producer. Worse,

the state's-rights distributors usually did not have access to the very best theatrical outlets. Some of these were owned outright by the large production and distribution companies, and many more of them were locked into exclusive agreements with the major firms. And the final problem, with film and money changing hands so often, was that there were just that many more opportunities to cheat the original producer.

Despite all these disadvantages, Disney had no real choice if he wished to retain control of his product, and apparently Powers' distribution offer was gratefully received by a man tired of worrying over money and deals at a moment when he sensed that he had, for the first time, a real hit. Disney's main purpose at this point was to exploit his sudden advantage, to get more films made and before the public. He seemed to sense that it was more and better cartoons rather than large immediate returns that would ultimately establish the name of Walt Disney.

So he closed with Powers and got to work while still in New York on the creation of scores for his two unreleased silent Mickey Mouse films, *Plane Crazy* and *Gallopin' Gaucho*, as well as for a brand-new vehicle for the mouse, *The Opry House*. Again he turned to his native Kansas City for talent he could rely on—a faithful theatre organist who had previously lent him money was brought east to score the films. By the time he left New York early in 1929, Disney had a package of four films ready for release. When these went into national distribution, their cumulative impact was simply tremendous; so great, in fact, that Disney was emboldened to attempt an animated short without Mickey or Minnie.

That picture was *The Skeleton Dance*, the first in the famous series of Silly Symphonies. However primitive it may seem to a modern audience, it then represented an extremely important advance for the animated cartoon. In *The Opry House*, Disney had already moved musically beyond "Yankee Doodle"; in that cartoon, Mickey and company cavort to a Rachmaninoff prelude. Now he decided to animate Saint-Saëns' *Danse Macabre* (with a few bars of some other serious music—notably "In the Hall of the Mountain King" from Grieg's *Peer Gynt* suite—thrown in). Obviously this was not suitable music for Mickey and his gang, whose activities were firmly located against an American small-town and country background. So Disney had to break with the most firmly held of all the conventions of animation—using animals as the principal characters.

It is difficult to say just what cultural influence was

driving Disney at this time. Although he had studied the violin briefly as a boy, he had no real musical knowledge nor, indeed, standards. This is obvious from his cheerful chopping and bowdlerizing of music, not only in *The Skeleton Dance* but in all of his later work, not excluding his mightiest effort at uplift, *Fantasia*. (Indeed, when he was working on *Fantasia* he so felt his lack of musical training that he subscribed to a box at the Hollywood Bowl concerts, where, he recalled to a co-worker, he invariably fell asleep, lulled by the music and the warmth of the polo coat he liked to wrap around himself in those days.) One suspects that Disney's desire to bring serious music into an area where it had not previously penetrated was based on several considerations. First was his commercially intelligent desire to differentiate his work from that of less adventurous competitors. Then there was the technical challenge that complex music presented to the animator. As early as 1925 he had made a short in which a cartoon character seemed to conduct a theatre's live orchestra from the screen. He had also toyed with the notion of supplying musical cue sheets to theatre musicians so his silent shorts could be properly accompanied. In addition, there was, perhaps, his vaguely defined yet keenly felt yearning for "the finer things." His father, as Disney once said, "would go for anything that was educational," and Disney himself proved throughout his career that he was chipped off much the same block (though his ideas of what was educational were often eccentric). Finally, there was his own shrewd sense that sound—as he felt it could be used—was the basis of his new success.

To understand this point, one must take a closer look at Mickey Mouse. There is no more useful tool for this purpose than the print of the silent version of *Plane Crazy* owned by the Museum of Modern Art in New York. The film is not a bad piece of animation when judged by the standards of its time. Particularly in the anthropomorphizing of inaminate objects, like the airplane in which Mickey takes Minnie up for a ride, it is quite good. That machine, like others that followed it, actually registers emotions—it strains forward in anticipation of action and cowers when it sees obstacles looming ahead. The construction of the story, too, is superior to that found in most competing cartoons. It is, like most silent comedies, live or animated, nothing more nor less than a string of physically perilous disasters, each more absurd and more dangerous than the last but all stemming from a perfectly reasonable premise—the natural desire of a young swain to prove his masculine prowess by taking his girl friend for a ride in an airplane that he has designed and constructed. When, at the end, the mice extricate themselves from their assorted perils (Minnie parachutes to safety with a great display of patched bloomers; Mickey successfully makes a forced landing), it is clear to the viewer that he has seen a work of talent and intelligence, however crude.

One also observes that Disney and his people made shrewd use of satire by giving Mickey's hair a Lindberghian ruffle when he stands in his plane taking bows for his achievements. One is impressed, too, by the fact that, faced with the need to create an original cartoon, Disney had the wit to draw upon his own experience for subject matter. His recollections of the mice in his Kansas City workshop inspired the main character, his rural boyhood supplied the barnyard setting for background, and his understanding of the typically American urge to tinker and invent provided the film's psychological motivation.

But having observed all this, one is still bound to conclude that the mouse, as originally conceived and as silently presented, was a very shaky basis for the empire that was to come. As *Time* observed in 1954 in a biographical sketch of Mickey, "he was a skinny little squeaker with matchstick legs, shoe button eyes and a long pointy nose. His teeth were sharp and fierce when he laughed, more like a real mouse's than they are today. . . ." His disposition matched his appearance. He was quick and cocky and cruel, at best a fresh and bratty kid, at worst a diminutive and sadistic monster—like most of the other inhabitants of that primitive theatre of cruelty that was the animated cartoon. Five minutes with the mouse, however diverting, were quite enough. His amazing—indeed, impossible—voyagings in various guises were often amusing enough in their broad conception and they supported some excellent comic situations, but the truth is that at the outset it was the witty, constantly surprising use of sound to punctuate the stories, and the technical genius of the animation, that brought the best laughs.

This is nowhere more obvious than in *Steamboat Willie*. In it the mouse has, if anything, regressed as a character; he represents nothing more than the spirit of pure, amoral, very boyish mischief. Employed as an assistant to the villainous Peg-Leg Pete, he takes it upon himself to rescue Minnie, who appears to be the riverboat's sole passenger, from Pete's lustful advances. In the course of the ensuing chase, the mice find themselves among a group of domestic animals housed in the boat's hold. A goat nibbles some sheet music, Minnie cranks his tail as if it were the handle of a street organ, and out of his mouth comes "Turkey in the Straw." There then pours forth a formidable concert—in which a cow's teeth are played as if they were a xylophone, a nursing sow is converted into a bagpipe, and so on—in a marvel-

ously inventive and rapidly paced medley. The gags are not very subtle ones and, indeed, there is something a little shocking about the ferocity with which Mickey squeezes, bangs, twists, and tweaks the anatomy of the assembled creatures in his mania for music. But even today the effect of the sequence is catchy; in 1928 it must have been truly stunning.

What Disney had understood was that sound was not merely an addition to the movies but a force that would fundamentally transform them. He became the first movie maker to fuse sight and sound successfully, making them absolutely "co-expressible," as one critic explained it, with neither dominant or carrying more than its fair share of the film's weight. The concert in *Steamboat Willie* presages those intricate animation sequences that were to be the high points of his studio's work in years to come—a rendition of the *William Tell* overture continuing aloft in a twister in the Mickey Mouse short *The Band Concert* (1935), the housecleaning sequence in *Snow White*, the ballet of the hippopotamuses (to "The Dance of the Hours") in *Fantasia*. All are infinitely more sophisticated than Mickey's musical interlude in *Willie*, but their basic appeal is the same: to ear and eye, "they come out right." It would be preposterous to assume that Disney knew consciously where he was going in *Steamboat Willie*. He, too, simply liked things to come out right. But he knew better than his distributors did where the appeal of his films lay. They were convinced that Mickey Mouse was, like other leading cartoon characters, an exploitable personality, a "star" of a sort. Disney realized that it was technique, not personality, that drew the audiences.

Even though within a few months Mickey Mouse cartoons were getting billing on marquees, an almost unprecedented commercial tribute for a short subject, Disney was determined not to be trapped by his own mouse. By May of 1929—with the Mickey series barely under way—he had *The Skeleton Dance* ready for release. He sent the print off to Powers, who rejected it, telling Disney to stick to mice. He then took it to a friend who ran one of the theatres in the United Artists Los Angeles chain and got him to show *The Skeleton Dance* to a morning audience. One of the man's assistants sat with Disney during the screening and, when it was over, told him he could not possibly recommend it for regular showings, despite the fact that most of the customers liked it, because it was simply too gruesome. Still Disney pressed on. Tracking down a film salesman in a pool hall, he wangled a showing of his cartoon at the Carthay Circle Theatre, one of the most prestigious houses in Los Angeles. It was a hit and collected an excellent set of notices. Back the film went to Powers, this time with its West Coast reviews and the advice to get it seen by "Roxy" Rothafel. The famous showman liked it, put it into the Roxy Theatre, and found himself with such a successful short on his hands that he held it over through several changes of feature.

The Skeleton Dance has no story and no characters at all. It is set in a graveyard in the smallest hours of the night, when the skeletons emerge from their graves and vaults, dance together for a few minutes, and then, with the coming of dawn, climb back into their resting places. It is such an innocently conceived movie that it is hard to imagine its frightening anyone. Yet its grotesque quality must have seemed remarkably advanced to audiences that had seldom seen such sophisticated iconography at the movies.

Its dividends for Disney were not to be counted merely in box-office terms. Indeed, after a year of work and the completion of twenty-one films, Disney had little to show for his efforts economically. What *The Skeleton Dance* did was provide diversity, forming the basis for a series of films in which, free of the artistic conventions and story lines imposed on him by Mickey and his "gang," he could experiment with techniques. He even had one or two large financial successes with the Silly Symphonies, though at first his distributors insisted on a very strange billing: "Mickey Mouse Presents a Walt Disney Silly Symphony."

Meantime, it was becoming clear to Disney that his deal with Powers was not working out. Throughout this year of extraordinarily hard labor, he and his brother had been unable to get a full financial report from their man in New York. Instead, he would send them checks for three or four thousand dollars, which was enough to keep going but nothing like what the Disneys felt they should be getting for their widely acclaimed Mickey series. Even more disturbing was the rumor that Powers was trying to make off with Ub Iwerks. Powers had been led to believe, not totally erroneously, that Iwerks was the real talent at the Disney studio. If he could be lured away and set up in his own shop, Powers hoped he might find himself in much the position Disney was now in—a producer with a possibly unlimited future. In any case, Powers planned to use the threat of hiring Iwerks as a way of bringing Disney to satisfactory terms on a new contract. Disney and his wife again entrained for New York, this time taking a lawyer. In Powers they found a man who had outsmarted himself. He had not counted on the mouse's great success. Planning Disney's creation as no more than a loss leader in the promotion of his sound system, Powers had neglected to make a tight contract with Disney; it ran for only one year, with no renewal option. From the moment Powers realized that Mickey Mouse was far more valuable than his Cinephone, he had been trying, legally or extralegally, to bind Disney to him.

Now Powers' strategy became clear. He greeted Disney by showing him a telegram from his Los Angeles representative indicating that Iwerks had just signed a contract with Powers to produce a cartoon series of his own. He also refused to let Disney examine his books to determine what money was due him, unless he agreed to a new contract. Of course, Powers informed him coolly, he was free to undertake a costly, time-consuming court fight for a fair accounting. On the other hand, Powers assured the young producer that he did not wish to appear unreasonable. If Disney agreed to sign the new contract, not only would he receive the sums due him for his last year's labor, but Powers would tear up his new contract with Iwerks and agree to pay Disney $2,500 a week in the future. Disney asked for a little time to think things over, and he later recalled that it was not until he was walking back to his hotel that the full magnitude of the $2,500-a-week offer struck him. It was more money than anyone had ever mentioned to him before, and he remembered muttering the figure aloud, to the wonderment of various passersby. The impressiveness of the sum was undoubtedly a mistake on the part of Powers, as indeed was his whole shabby strategy, since it was based on a fundamental misreading of his man. The $2,500 figure had the effect of confirming Disney's own estimation of the value of what he was doing. It also indicated to him that he was not without bargaining strength himself.

Before he left home his brother had told him that he must obtain an immediate cash advance from Powers in order to keep the studio operating, and so, when he returned to the distributor for further discussions, he casually mentioned the need for cash. Anxious to indicate his good will, Powers drew a check for $5,000, and Disney stalled him until it cleared. Then he promptly broke off the negotiations. He made no attempt to retain Iwerks, who, with Powers' backing, set up his own shop and, for a while, produced a series called *Flip the Frog*. It did not catch

on, perhaps because Iwerks lacked the one talent everyone who ever worked for Disney agrees that Walt had in abundance—that of story editor. He certainly lacked the Disney brothers' ability to control costs and to cope with the fast-talking financial world beyond the studio door. Within a few years Iwerks was back at work for Disney, where he has remained ever since—on a business-only basis. Witnesses report that Disney carefully looked the other way when passing Iwerks on the lot or, at best, spoke to him in monosyllables. Iwerks' mechanical genius was of enormous value to Disney, but his moment of disloyalty was never forgotten.

After extricating himself from Powers, Disney had to find a new distributor. The man he finally settled with was Harry Cohn, the president of Columbia Pictures. This time Disney had no trouble striking a bargain that allowed him to retain the ownership of his films and the independence of his studio. The trouble was that his drive for an improved product continued to push costs up. At the time he signed with Columbia, a Disney short cost $5,400 to produce. By late 1931 he was spending $13,500 on each little film and doing no better than breaking even on them. Each cartoon barely paid for the next one. Worried about costs but always a perfectionist, Disney was driving himself relentlessly in the time-honored tradition of the American success ethic. He recalled later that he often took his wife out for dinner, then suggested dropping in to the studio to do a few minutes' work. She would stretch out on a couch in his office and fall asleep, and he would plunge on at his job, losing track of time until he glanced at his watch and found that it was after one o'clock in the morning. When he woke his wife and she asked what time it was, he would tell her it was only ten thirty. He claimed she never discovered the truth.

Also at about this time the problems presented by Mickey's character became extremely frustrating. The mouse more or less fitted the description of him written in 1934 by no less a literary figure than E. M. Forster, who found Mickey "energetic without being elevated" and added that "no one has ever been softened after seeing Mickey or has wanted to give away an extra glass of water to the poor. He is never sentimental, indeed there is a scandalous element in him which I find most restful." The trouble was that some people were scandalized rather than refreshed by Mickey's style, and the popularity he did attain, as the critic Gilbert Seldes said in 1932, had "some of the elements of a fad, where it joins the

kewpie and the Teddy Bear." To have started a fad was obviously not good enough for Disney. Mickey had to become both more verbal and somewhat softer in manner if he was to be a symbol that could outlast the shifts of fashion.

Although he recognized the necessity for the change, transforming Mickey's character seemed to disturb Disney almost as if it were his own personality that was being tampered with. It also presented him with purely aesthetic decisions that were painful. Likable as Mickey was becoming, his new sweet self was as difficult to build a cartoon around as his old sharp self had been. He was still not funny in and of himself—he was merely unfunny in a different, though perhaps more generally appealing, way. (This humorlessness, as well as his naïveté and his enthusiasm for projects, were perhaps traits the mouse inherited from Disney, who insisted that he had a sense of humor and scorned anyone who lacked one, but who was never known to

have uttered a genuinely funny remark in his life.)

Disney apparently saw as early as 1931 that Mickey was simply not very adaptable. As he later said, he was "trapped with the mouse . . . stuck with the character." Mickey "couldn't do certain things—they would be out of character. And Mickey was on a pedestal—I would get letters if he did something wrong. I got worried about relying on a character like the mouse—you wear it out, you run dry." The answer for him was diversification. "We got Pluto and the duck. The duck could blow his top. Then I tied Pluto and Donald together. The stupid things Pluto would do, along with the duck, gave us an outlet for our gags."

The process of developing new characters, however, was slow. As of 1931, Disney had in addition to Mickey and Minnie only the villainous Peg-Leg Pete and a couple of rubber-limb-and-circle combinations known as Clarabelle Cow and Horace Horsecollar, who were serviceable but not memorable. It is true that a Pluto-type dog had appeared as one of a pair of bloodhounds

WALT DISNEY: *Myth and Reality*

Not long before he died, Walt Disney was asked to name the most rewarding experience of his life. The response was blunt and brief: "The whole damn thing. The fact that I was able to build an organization and hold it." His words may seem surprising. To the public at large he was an avuncular Horatio Alger character, a spinner of sweet tales for children, a man whose taste and morality comfortably reflected those of the middle-class American majority. This image was carefully nurtured by a corps of press agents and sycophants as competent and energetic as any in Hollywood—men as skillful in turning aside questions and questioners that might damage that image as they were in propagating it. In fact, however, Walt Disney was a grouchy, inarticulate, withdrawn man. Intellectually and emotionally he remained a child, but he was anything but childlike when it came to managing and directing the only thing he greatly cared about—his business or, to use the phrase favored by his publicity department, his "magic kingdom."

Poorly educated, the product of a childhood no objective observer could possibly describe as happy, bankrupt in his early twenties, he was a driven and

a driving man, determined to "make it" in a way more honored in the folklore of our capitalistic system than in its practice. If he had had his way, for example, Disney would have financed the growth of his enterprises solely out of profits; he would never have had anything to do with outsiders like banks or stockholders, whom he tolerated with ill-disguised distrust. Everything that came out of his workshops was stamped with his name and, indeed, with his taste and personality, a practice which eventually drove most of his genuinely talented elves from his employ.

This egocentricity caused many problems. A man less insistent on maintaining absolute personal control of every aspect of his enterprise might have built faster and have made fewer difficulties for himself. But he could not have built better. And here the career of Disney and his studio following the birth of the mouse is significant. Adored by both intellectuals and children, winner of awards and fame for his creator, Mickey was a problem child. After a delightfully bratty beginning he matured into a terrible square, simply incapable of the kind of irreverent comic turns that a great comedian must master. Disney

felt, as he said, "locked in" by the mouse. From 1929 through 1937 he plowed all his profits and energy into unlocking innovations—more viable comic characters like Pluto and Donald Duck, the Silly Symphony series, and, most important of all, the attempt to create a feature-length cartoon, which culminated in *Snow White*.

Another man might have rested and consolidated his gains after the success of that film. Disney instead pressed forward and had three full-length features on the drawing boards of his expensive new studio when a strike—which he handled with inept repressiveness—and the beginning of World War II—which cut off his vital foreign markets—nearly cost him everything he had gained. Government contracts, mostly for training films, kept the studio running, but it took a decade for him to find a way out of his difficulties. In that time the intellectuals who had lavished praise and attention on him, as they previously had on Charlie Chaplin, deserted Disney. *Fantasia*, a rube's idea of what thinking men ought to like, left them cool, and such wartime propaganda outbursts as *Saludos Amigos*, not to mention Disney's labor record, sealed their aliena-

chasing Mickey in *The Chain Gang* in 1930, and that the same dog had appeared again with the mouse in *The Picnic*. He was known as Rover in that picture, however, and his useful presence was not apparent until late in 1931 when he acquired his appealing name and the beginnings of his marvelously eager, innocent, and therefore troublemaking identity. The duck did not arrive until 1934, when he had one line of dialogue ("Who—me? Oh, no! I got a bellyache!") in *The Wise Little Hen*. His genesis is interesting, however. It seems that Disney heard an obscure entertainer named Clarence Nash on a local radio show reciting "Mary Had a Little Lamb" as a girl duck. He discovered Nash was employed by a local dairy to put on shows for schools, hired him away, and then tried to create a character to match his duck voice. It was not until some unsung genius changed the duck's sex and temperament that Nash found his métier. He has been the voice of Donald Duck ever since. The other members of the stable (or "gang," as Disney people preferred to call it)—Chip and Dale, the team of comic chipmunks; Daisy Duck, Donald's inamorata; and Donald's nephews Huey, Louie, and Dewey—all came along several years after the duck.

Altogether this diversification of characters—the creation of new stars, one might call it—required most of a decade and was not therefore the immediate answer to Disney's problems. Nor did his stylistic innovations bring money rolling in. He clung steadfastly to the Silly Symphony series. About half of these were original material, and the other half were based on traditional folk tales, with a heavy reliance on Aesop. But until *The Three Little Pigs* became his biggest short-subject success in 1933-34, the series did not make a large, direct contribution to his financial progress. If anything, it was a drain.

A temporary solution to the problem of keeping Mickey fresh and amusing was to move him out of the sticks and into cosmopolitan environments and roles. The locales of his adventures throughout the nineteen

tion. Hurt, and hunkered down against the financial storm, Disney ended aesthetic experiment. The style and technique of his animated films remained forever fixed at the 1940 level, and Warner Brothers (with Bugs Bunny and company) soon surpassed him in humor and characterization, as United Productions of America (with Mr. Magoo and Gerald McBoing Boing) later surpassed him in style.

From 1950 on, however, Disney did not seem to care. He found there was infinitely more money to be made with his nature documentaries, which were well received, and his live-action adventures and situation comedies, most of which were beneath critical comment but which were extraordinarily profitable. His fearlessness about new technologies led him to try television when the rest of the movie industry was hoping that if they ignored it, it would go away. He used television as an enormously effective loss leader to promote his films and, shortly, his long-held dream—Disneyland.

As with all of his experiments, the Disneyland scheme produced more doubters than believers; as always, Disney bulled the project through. As a result of its success he passed, in the fifties, from being a marginal operator to being a mogul on the grand scale, presiding over an entertainment empire operating in every medium of communication known to man. Diversification gave Disney a stability unknown to firms working exclusively in movies and it led to potentially enormous profits in other real estate-*cum*-recreation ventures like the projected Disneyworld in Florida and the Mineral King ski resort in California. Volume of business soared in this period, as did Disney's personal worth.

In the early fifties he had had to borrow on a modest life insurance policy to finance planning for Disneyland; at about that time, he claimed to have only about a thousand dollars in the bank. When he died, his estate was worth twenty million dollars and also contained deferred payment and royalty arrangements of inestimable value. His wealth had at last caught up with his fame, yet he continued to live with ostentatious modesty. To associates he grew less approachable and more enigmatic than ever, though he continued to exercise personal control over the smallest details of the operation.

He remained suspicious of outsiders, strangely small-minded on questions of aesthetics and narrow-minded on morals, and deeply wedded to the propagation of the happy myth of small-town, turn-of-the-century virtue. At once the greatest entrepreneur of innovation the entertainment business had ever seen and a man nostalgic for a lost, perhaps never-existent past, he withdrew into the "magic kingdom" of his own creation where he could rule absolutely. His real nature remained a well-kept secret, and the public were as content with the folksy persona that Disney and his press agents gave them as they were with the studio's products. Indeed, now that he is gone they seem to miss the myth rather badly. The biggest problem facing the committee of more conventional, less colorful businessmen who have succeeded Disney is to destroy the cult of personality which, until a year and a half ago, most of them had worked so assiduously to build. If they succeed, the beautiful money machine which Disney labored so hard to build, and which reached perfection only recently, should continue to function without friction. It will be interesting to see how much it needed its founder's guiding hand and what capacity he built into it for self-perpetuation.—*R.S.*

thirties ranged from the South Seas to the Alps to the deserts of Africa. He was at various times a gaucho, teamster, explorer, swimmer, cowboy, fireman, convict, pioneer, taxi driver, castaway, fisherman, cyclist, Arab, football player, inventor, jockey, storekeeper, camper, sailor, Gulliver, boxer, exterminator, skater, polo player, circus performer, plumber, chemist, magician, hunter, detective, clock cleaner, Hawaiian, carpenter, driver, trapper, whaler, tailor, and Sorcerer's Apprentice. In short, he was Everyman and the Renaissance Man combined. As Forster said, "Mickey's great moments are moments of heroism, and when he carries Minnie out of the harem as a pot-plant or rescues her as she falls in foam . . . he reaches heights impossible for the entrepreneur."

Unfortunately, it was as an entrepreneur that the mouse finally found his most viable identity. By the mid-thirties he appeared more and more frequently as the manager and organizer of various events—and his "gang" more and more frequently carried the whole comic load. One cannot help but suspect that this was a reflection of Disney's strong identification with the mouse. By then Disney himself was occupied princi-

CULVER

pally as the manager, organizer, and co-ordinator of an organization that had grown from a handful of people to a complex of some 750 employees by 1937, when *Snow White* was in full production. The mouse was by this time rounder, sleeker, and far more human in appearance. And, like his creator, he was also more sober, sensible, and suburban in outlook—a better organized mouse. In fact, Mickey had grown up.

A Woman's Place CONTINUED FROM PAGE 11

another and a brighter course with matured powers. I know of no one whose life has such bright promise in it as yours."

Fanny hoped to fulfill that promise, as well as to keep those she had made before the altar to Pierce. It was to be nearly twenty-five years before she achieved the first hope. The other was doomed to tragic, total failure.

From the start of her married life, Fanny found herself "cabinn'd and confined." Pierce's family made it clear that they had strained their tolerance to its limit by admitting her to their circle. None of her "theatrical" friends were to be permitted to follow her in. The few Philadelphians to whom Fanny was attracted always turned out to be inadmissible on other grounds —political, for the most part. She was to be condemned to the company of people she found stupid, ignorant, and intolerably bigoted. (If the Butlers were social snobs, Fanny was an intellectual and moral snob of the same, or purer, water.) In no time at all she was suffering from a sort of spiritual starvation.

Fanny had suffered many things in her life, but never this particular sort of deprivation. She now had the solitude she had once craved, and yet she was appalled to find that she was unable to read or write or think—or even practice the piano. They had moved

into the country by this time (at Fanny's insistence), and Pierce had to be away for days at a time, which made the solitude even more intense. Even when he was there, he could not supply her intellectual needs.

He did his best to make her comfortable and content. When Fanny complained that she was "weary of her useless existence" and begged him to send her to England to await the birth of her child, he treated her as if she were herself a child, and assured her that her misery was "merely perverse fancies." For a while Fanny half-believed him and looked forward to some mystical change at the instant she became a mother, a new sense of fulfillment that would quiet her troubled spirit and strengthen the ties that bound her to Pierce.

Before there was time to test that faith, however, a rift had opened between Fanny and Pierce deep enough to dispel all hope of rapprochement. It seems incredible that Fanny did not know, when she married into the Butler clan, that its fortune was based on rice and cotton holdings in the Deep South, which was to say, on the labor of slaves; or that Pierce did not know that Fanny held strong convictions on the essential evil of slavery. When it finally dawned on Fanny that she was living in idleness at the expense of black men, women, and children, and that her husband was destined soon to be the master of some seven hundred such chattels, she was horrified and said so with dramatic eloquence.

Fanny's views on the question of slavery were the prevailing views of upper-class Englishmen of that day, intensified in her case by contact with New England antislavery intellectuals and in particular with the Unitarian saint, William Ellery Channing. It was his little book *Slavery* to which Fanny turned for guidance in the moral dilemma in which she found herself. Channing had called on Christian slaveholders to assume the responsibility of preparing their bondsmen for emancipation by conversion and education and the institution of a system of wages. Fanny proposed this to Pierce and his brother, reminding them that Channing was the acknowledged spiritual leader of the faith the Butler family professed.

Pierce, who still loved her, tried patiently to explain the fundamental financial facts of their life: that he had no choice but to continue in the way that had been laid out for him and to strive to be the best and most humane master possible. Fanny denied these imperatives. She would rather go back to earning her own bread on the stage than to continue a day longer "eating the bitter bread of slavery!" She was being anything but tactful, but she was suffering in ways that Pierce could not comprehend.

For Fanny was something very rare in the human species: a moral absolutist. She herself was only just beginning to be able to put into words the fact that "freedom of conscience . . . the power to pursue duty and right as she was able to conceive them was of more value to her than anything else beside." Fanny's sense of duty was to her literally "the vital part of life."

How completely Pierce failed to understand this was demonstrated when, required for business reasons to spend the winter of 1838–39 at his Georgia plantations, he let his family persuade him to take Fanny and the children (there was a second daughter by now) with him. Exposure to the "true facts," the Butlers assumed, would cure her of her wrong-headed notions about the Negro and show her the error of the abolitionist argument. It did, as might have been expected, just the reverse.

Fanny went to Georgia determined to carry out the Channing program—with or without Pierce's collaboration. The effect of her ministry (or perhaps it was simply her presence) was to stir what Pierce took for warning signs of mutiny. He felt himself obliged to order her to desist. But to look upon the spectacle of human degradation and suffering and be helpless to alleviate it was to Fanny an almost unbearable torment. She had to act, if only to put down on paper a record of what she saw and heard and smelled and felt.

For the first time since her marriage, she went back to her old habit of keeping a journal.

The result (combined with letters to antislavery friends in Massachusetts and in England) was *The Journal of a Residence on a Georgian Plantation, 1838–39*, a unique observation of the South's "peculiar institution" by a sensitive, intelligent woman who happened also to be a highly gifted writer. Even before her return to the North, Fanny was being urged by abolitionists who had seen some of her letters to let them be published, to "bear her witness" against the flood of proslavery propaganda then issuing from presses in both the North and the South.

Fanny and Pierce quarrelled bitterly and protractedly over the matter. Her Georgia journal became the *place d'armes* on which an even more fundamental struggle between them was carried on. Pierce absolutely forbade her to publish any part of the document, but it was a Pyrrhic victory. Fanny was driven to express her convictions in other ways that damaged him just as seriously. His love for her was the first casualty of the battle, and he now looked forward to nothing but being rid of her before she ruined him, not only socially and financially (for Pierce imagined that her influence might yet spark a slave revolt on his Georgia properties) but morally as well. Their estrangement and the sustained tension between them was driving him to seek consolation with other women. But Fanny, who had once asked him to "send her away before the bonds of affection should have time to knit" between her and her daughters, now refused stubbornly to be parted from the girls.

Pennsylvania's marriage law, based on the old common law, held that "husband and wife were a legal unity and the rights of both parties to that unity were executed by the husband alone. Consequently . . . he was the sole legal guardian and in effect the sole legal parent of the minor children of the marriage." Fanny knew as well as Pierce that they ought to separate, but she had discovered that she could not afford freedom at this price. Also, under this same law, any money or property that Fanny might inherit or earn was Pierce's to administer as he saw fit. He could, if he were so disposed, withhold from her everything but shelter and food. And if she went back to the stage, he could take and keep every dollar she earned.

It took five nightmarish years to resolve this impasse. The details of the private war between them became public during the divorce proceedings. (They are available in the rare book collection of the Library of Congress in a small volume entitled *Mrs. Butler's Narrative and Pierce Butler's Answer*.) What is set down in these two biased accounts is essentially a series of moves by Pierce to provoke Fanny to leave him of her own volition, and countermoves by Fanny designed to retain contact with her children, who had by now become the object of her obsessive affection. The children, of course, suffered even more deeply than the combatants.

At one point, while the Butlers were in England on a prolonged and turbulent visit, Pierce hired a governess to supersede Fanny in the care and education of Sally and little Fan. His excuse was that Fanny had left his house, presumably for good. Less than a month later she forced her way back in, but the governess was not discharged, nor was Fanny's authority re-established. Fanny and Pierce began living in embittered separation under the same roof, receiving and accepting social invitations—sometimes to the same affair —as if they were strangers. It was the talk of London and the source of terrible embarrassment to Fanny's family and friends.

When the couple finally returned to Philadelphia, it was to live in separate rented quarters in the same house. After a time, Fanny demanded and Pierce agreed to a separate maintenance agreement that provided that she was to have "uninterrupted intercourse with her children." But not long afterward, Pierce moved into a house of his own, and soon she was complaining through lawyers and mutual friends that the agreement had been violated, that she was in effect entirely cut off from her children.

Pierce was by now convinced that he was dealing with a malicious madwoman who was undermining the authority of the governess, emotionally scarring the two little girls in unforgivable ways, and playing the wronged wife and mother so as to damage his own character more cruelly than calumny could have done. He began to lose control of himself, to fall prey to

Fanny Kemble's 1829 debut at Covent Garden was noted in the programme as "her first appearance on any stage."

paranoid suspicions, and to descend to actions that shamed him even as he committed them, such as selling her horse after she defied his injunction to stop riding by herself.

Fanny was suffering indescribably. She was reduced to something close to beggary, and every cent that was doled out to her was tainted with the agony of black men and women, many of whom she had known and, in many cases, loved. Yet she could not speak out on their behalf. To secure visiting privileges with her daughters, she had been forced to promise in writing that she would not declare her sentiments on slavery in any public manner. She had promised not to publish anything without her husband's approval—not even a poetic tragedy—and not to return to the stage. But after all these concessions, she was still effectually deprived of her children, reduced to loitering about the streets of Philadelphia to catch a glimpse of them on their daily walks. Once when she accosted them and the governess ordered them to pass on without speaking, Fanny lost her head and ran after them, calling their names and sobbing aloud.

The situation had become a scandal, and at last a Unitarian minister, the Reverend William Furness (Fanny's friend and fellow Channingite), interceded. He pleaded with Pierce to re-admit Fanny into his household for her sake and the girls', and for the sake of his own public image. Pierce reluctantly agreed, but on conditions that Fanny could never in her right mind have accepted.

There were stipulations that she was not to keep up an acquaintance with any person of whom Pierce disapproved; that she cut off all intercourse—even by letter—with the Sedgwick family, which included both her best American woman friend and her legal adviser; that in correspondence with her family she cease to mention Pierce or any circumstance that occurred in his house. And, as an afterthought, Pierce amended the last condition to read that she was not even to speak to him! "Any communication that I may have to make to her, shall be made in writing." This, while she was to be living in his house and eating at his table.

He insisted that he was simply taking steps to defend his reputation and that of those whom, like the governess and the children, it was his duty to protect. Perhaps he hoped that Fanny would reject the conditions and give up the fight. But for six incredible months she tried to abide by them, living in what amounted to solitary confinement.

Toward the end, she wondered if she was indeed as mad as Pierce thought her. She considered suicide and drew back from it, fearing that death might prove another trap. As she wrote in one of the poems into which she poured out her anguish: *"The spirit may not lose its deeper curse./It finds no death in the whole universe."*

The struggle might have gone on until one or both of the principals was destroyed, if Fanny had not finally become aware of what was happening to Sally and Fan. She had watched their bewildered misery turn slowly into resentment of her, and now she saw their health, physical and mental, being undermined.

The breaking point came in 1845, in the middle of an August heat wave. Pierce had chosen this time to have his town house renovated. He sent the girls to a farm in the country and the governess to a watering place, made other housing arrangements for himself, and left Fanny to endure as best she might the dust, noise, and confusion of the dismantled house. When she defied his ban and followed the girls to the farm, he retaliated by bringing them back to the stifling city. The next time she saw them, they were hysterical and half sick. She had had all she could stand; when her family urged her to return to England, she agreed.

Fanny sailed for London in September, having borrowed the passage money from friends, who did not expect to see her again.

After a brief visit with her father, she took refuge with her sister and brother-in-law, the Edward Sartorises, who were living in Rome. Their affectionate generosity and her own enduring vitality worked together to perform a miracle of healing.

The first sign of returning life was a journal she began to keep, not as before for herself or friends, but for eventual sale to a publisher. Fanny was beginning to look ahead, to face the problem of how she was to earn her living and perhaps her children's as well. For Pierce's fortunes were entering a long decline into eventual bankruptcy, brought on in part by his own fecklessness, in part by the vagaries of the cotton market.

Whatever she wrote, she was able to sell. Her *Year of Consolation,* as the Italian journal was called, was contracted for even before it was finished. But one did not support oneself on the proceeds of volumes of collected letters and reminiscences. What else could she do? There was the theatre. But would it accept its prodigal daughter, now that she was neither young nor beautiful? The Kembles knew well how uncharitable the profession was to portly leading ladies and men, no matter how glamourous their youth had been.

Fanny's sister suggested that she give concert readings of Shakespeare's plays, without scenery or costumes, taking all the parts, as their father was doing. Fanny was tempted. She knew it would not tax her to play all the roles, because she had always done it in

her mind when she was preparing her own. Furthermore, she would be using only those of her talents that had not been affected by time. Her dancer's grace was gone, but her voice was not.

But was the audience available for such performances large enough for two Kembles? Fanny decided it was not. Instead, she went back to England, forced herself to lose thirty pounds in twice that many days, and let it be known that she was again available to play any of her old roles—except the ingénues—at something close to her old salary. She was canny and courageous enough to act on the assumption that it was all or nothing, for "no one would hire a Kemble to play Nerissa or Juliet's Nurse." It was a brave gamble.

Offers were slow in coming. The first was from the management of the Princess Theatre in London. It was so meager that she knew it was meant to be refused. The next—after a dismaying interval—was from a theatre in Manchester. The terms were better, but the role was that of a twenty-year-old heroine in a melodrama, and Fanny was not at all pleased with the quality of the cast. Still, it was an opportunity, and there might not be another.

She was almost as certain of failure as she had been when she ventured out for the first time on the stage of Covent Garden. And she was just as mistaken. The audience, some of whom had journeyed all the way up from London, cheered her to the echo. Unbelievably, she was back where she had left off.

Before that season was over, she was the leading lady of the Princess Theatre Company, playing opposite the great William Macready, at a salary which was adequate if not flattering. She was delighted to be back in the city where she felt most nearly at home, but not delighted with the work that kept her there. Of Macready she complained that:

He growls and prowls, and roams and foams, about the stage, in every direction, like a tiger in his cage, so that I never know on what side of me he means to be; and keeps up a perpetual snarling and grumbling ... so that I never feel quite sure that he *has done,* and that it is my turn to speak.

She also objected to the Macready repertory, which included comparatively little Shakespeare and a great many shoddy, bombastic melodramas.

Obviously, her distaste for the profession of acting had not lessened with the years. But it did enable her to support herself and to lay something by toward the cottage she hoped to buy in Massachusetts, to which she would bring Sally and Fan when the day of reunion came. Still another hope was beginning to grow in her: that somewhere—not in her present pursuit—

she might still find the fulfillment for which her spirit yearned.

Then, in her second season, her father decided quite suddenly to retire. He turned over to her not only the field of concert reading of Shakespeare, but also his carefully pruned and tested versions of most of the plays. The "bright scattered fragments" formed into the new "curious, beautiful, and mystical pattern" for which she had been waiting, and she felt herself called in a truly religious sense.

Before her first public reading, she made a pilgrimage to the little church at Stratford on Avon. "I have told [the reader] how curiously affected I was while standing by his grave," she later wrote in a memoir, ". . . how I was suddenly overcome with sleep (my invariable refuge under great emotion or excitement), and how I prayed to be allowed to sleep for a little while on the altar steps of the chancel, beside his bones: the power of association was certainly strong in me then, but his bones *are* there, and above them streamed a warm and brilliant sunbeam, fit emblem of his vivifying spirit."

The reading was to be in a small hall at Highgate, and she had chosen *The Tempest*. A few of her London friends insisted on coming, but for the most part it was to be an audience of strangers, "all ages, all kinds, all conditions of people." She supervised all the arrangements with meticulous care, so that nothing would distract from the words she would be speaking. There was a low platform at one end where she would be seated before a hanging of red damask; no furniture but a chair for her, a table for her book, and two clusters of candles on either side. She chose a dress of white satin, with a single flower at her breast.

From the moment she opened her book and began, Fanny was aware of a current flowing between her poet and those who received his message. The current swelled and swirled and carried all before it, until it seemed to erupt in a waterspout of applause. The audience was on its feet, clapping and stamping and cheering, knowing as surely as she did that she had found her place, her pattern, her true calling at last. The London critics were as enthusiastic and grateful as the audience.

As the terrible, wonderful year of 1848 began, with storms of liberty sweeping across Europe and the Chartists shaking the pillars of the British Establishment, Fanny was living at the epicenter, revelling in the excitement of history in the making. She had six weeks of solid bookings ahead of her, enough to pay for the trip to America and the cottage Catharine Sedgwick had found for her in Lenox. She was impatient to be there, to see—or at least to have fresh news of—her daughters. Friends who made inquiries about them could learn only that they were in boarding school. They advised Fanny to come and open a direct negotiation with Pierce for some sort of reasonable compromise.

She intended to do that when the season was over. But just as it began, she was served with a subpoena to appear before the court of common pleas in Philadelphia to defend herself against Pierce's suit for divorce on the grounds of "wilful and malicious desertion."

Fanny cancelled her engagements (including a royal command performance) and sailed for Boston. There she consulted friends, among them Charles Sumner, the abolitionist senator. It may well have been on his advice that she decided to base her defense on the argument that Pierce's ". . . prohibition of my remaining with my children . . . coupled with his other acts and his declarations, was as clear an expulsion of me from his house as there could be short of one accompanied by physical violence." She also contended that, while she had left with "the assent and license" of her husband, she would have been justified in leaving without them by "personal indignities [that] rendered [my] condition intolerable and life burdensome."

It would have been a stronger and more conventional case if she had alleged even a single act of physical mistreatment, for mental cruelty had no legal status at the time. But Fanny would not make the charge, probably because it would have been untrue.

To support her contentions, Fanny added to her plea for a jury trial her detailed *Narrative*, which, although the judges would not admit it as evidence, was widely published by the newspapers, many of which came to her defense. In addition, she retained as her lawyer the renowned Rufus Choate, a courtroom performer who could draw and move an audience as strongly in his way as Fanny could in hers. Since Choate's fee was high, Fanny contracted for a series of readings to raise the money.

Pierce did not exercise his legal prerogative of impounding her earnings. He may have considered it; he was desperately afraid of Choate and tried to hire Daniel Webster to oppose him. But any such move against Fanny would have prejudiced his case, not only in the eyes of his peers, but also in the eyes of the three judges on whose good opinion his fate would depend.

When the hearing began in early December, everyone who could squeeze into the courtroom was there—except Fanny. The Boston and New York papers sent reporters to take down every point Choate made, for there was consensus that more was at stake here than Fanny Butler's maternal rights.

THEATRE

For the Benefit of
MR. SIMPSON,

On which occasion, the following distinguished Performers, have
politely tendered their valuable services,

Miss Fanny Kemble,
Mrs. Austin,
Miss Clara Fisher,
Mr. Kemble,
Mr. Sinclair.
Signora Ferrero,

Doors Open at 7 o'clock & performance will commence precisely
at 1-2 past 7 o'clock.

On Monday Even'g, June 24,
Will be performed the new Play of the

Hunchback.

By James Sheridan Knowles, Esq.

Sir Thomas Clifford,	-			**Mr. Kemble.**
Master Walter,	....	....	....	Mr. Clarke
Lord Tinsel,	....	....	....	Richings
Master Wilford,	....	....		Barry
Modus,	....	....	....	Simpson
Master Heartwell,	....	:...	....	Blakeley
Gaylove,	....	....	....	Keppell
Fathom,	....	....	.	Placide
Thomas,	....	....	....	Povey
Stephen.	....	....	....	Nexsen
Williams,	....	....	....	Harvey
Simpson,	....	....	....	Bancker
Waiter,	....	....	....	Johnson
Holdwell,	....	....	....	Collet
Servant,	....	....	....	King
Julia,	-			**Miss Fanny Kemble.**
Helen,	...	....		Mrs. Sharpe

Fanny received top billing in The Hunchback,
performed in 1833 at New York's Park Theatre.

Choate did not disappoint his audience. After he
had emotionally charged the proceedings with the
plight of a mother who found she had no right under
the law of the land to perform those functions which
moral law demanded of her, he moved on to suggest
—very delicately but unmistakably—that the old
common law was unjust and ought to be revised. He
realized that such a change was beyond the power of
the three judges, but he knew that the hundreds who
heard him and thousands who would read him could
and would initiate change in their own time.

It took a month for the court to reach its decision:
that there was, in Mrs. Butler's countercharge, an issue
of fact (which Pierce's counsel had denied)) and that
the case must be tried before a jury. This made it
possible that Fanny might "win"—that the divorce
might be denied and the intolerable *status quo ante*
be resumed.

What happened next was anticlimactic but hardly
inexplicable in view of what each of the contestants
now stood to lose—and to gain. A compromise was
negotiated. Pierce permitted the two girls to spend
part of the summer with their mother, visiting them

himself only once and only for a few hours. For her
part, when the case came up for trial the following
September, Fanny did not contest the divorce.

If Fanny ever wrote down her reasons for this change
of heart and strategy, she later destroyed the record.
But it seems obvious that by giving up her daughters
for a few years she could win the right to her own
independence and secure their love. Nothing but a
revision in the law could have restored them to her
before their majority, and laws are not changed by a
single pleading, even by a Rufus Choate.

As it turned out, five years after Choate's inspired
defense the Pennsylvania assembly did act to amend
the statutes governing the position of married women.
The change was small but significant, for it granted to
a woman whose husband neglects her or refuses to
provide for her the right to whatever money she could
earn as a "sole trade." She also secured rights over her
children, should their father fail to care for them.

Fanny must have felt some sense of accomplishment,
some small part in the legislative victory, but she had
not spent those five years waiting for it. She was keeping herself too busy to feel her loneliness, travelling
about the non-slave states reading Shakespeare. She
did not make it easy for herself by reading only the
better known and more popular plays. To the frequent dismay of her managers, she insisted on a fairly
rigid sequence of twenty-four of the master's works.
Nevertheless, a generation of Americans preferred
Fanny's reading of Shakespeare to a full-cast performance, and she counted among her devotees such diverse spirits as Henry James, Walt Whitman, and
Henry Longfellow, who even wrote her a sonnet of
gratitude.

In 1856, Sally Butler turned twenty-one and went to
England with her mother for several months before
returning to Philadelphia to marry Dr. Owen Wister.
In 1859, Fan came of age, and she too chose to join her
mother abroad. Fanny's long purgatory was over; she
had both her girls again at last. Then the shadow of
war fell across her newfound happiness.

The election of Abraham Lincoln brought the
United States to the brink of disunion and armed conflict, and to Fanny's dismay she discovered that her
daughters differed as sharply as had she and Pierce on
the same issues. Once again she was forced to make a
choice between duty and love. For it was young Fan
who sided with her father and the South. For Fanny
to express her own passionate partisanship for the
Union and the antislavery cause was to risk alienating,
if not forfeiting, the daughter whose presence she had
just rewon. Fanny was not as headstrong—or perhaps
as heart-strong—as in the old days. She vacillated for
nearly two years.

The British Tory circles in which Fanny was living at this time were for the most part sympathetic to the Confederacy. As the armies of the South won battle after battle in the opening months of 1862, what Fanny heard over dinner tables and in drawing rooms convinced her that England was moving toward recognition of the Confederacy. Gladstone was cheered in Parliament when he said that "Jefferson Davis and other leaders of the Confederacy have made an army . . . and what is more important . . . they have made a nation!" If the Confederate cotton loan caught on in Britain's financial circles, the government might intervene to break the North's blockade of the cotton-shipping ports.

Fanny was doing her best to conceal or control her feelings, but it was becoming more and more difficult. She began to speak out, trying to disabuse some of her influential friends of their sentimental notions about Southern slavery. But few listened or were convinced by her emotional harangues. At last, toward the end of 1862, she decided that she must take some decisive action, she must strike some sort of blow.

She went back to her unpublished Georgia journal, which the abolitionists had once begged her to let them make into a weapon. Was it too late? Mrs. Stowe's fictionalized account of the same facts was changing public opinion in some circles. Might Fanny's factual account perhaps have an equivalent effect in those influential circles where British policy was made?

Still she hesitated, trying to assess whether the effect to be achieved outweighed the sacrifice required. Undoubtedly she talked with Fan about it, and what the girl said may be guessed from the fact that she left England and joined her father a little while after Fanny's final decision to submit the manuscript for publication. Perhaps Fanny's choice was eased by the knowledge that Sally and her husband were staunch Unionists and antislavery moderates and that she would not be cutting herself off from both her children this time. But what counted, as before, was the power to pursue duty and right as she perceived them.

Her book was a best seller on both sides of the ocean. It shocked prudes by its frankness as much as it angered supporters of the South, but it was read and discussed and debated everywhere. It was bitterly attacked by some critics, highly praised by others. The *Atlantic Monthly* called it "the first ample, lucid, faithful, detailed account, from the actual headquarters of a slave plantation in this country, of the workings of the system." Another critic concluded: "A sadder book the human hand never wrote."

Today, a century after its publication, there is still some debate among Civil War scholars as to whether Fanny's "pen of burning gold" drew blood or not. Her admirers claim it changed the balance of forces in Britain and therefore altered the course of the war; others insist that it had little effect, that it came too late (May, 1863, in London; two months later in New York), after the tide had already turned in favor of the North. Some maintain and others deny that portions of it were read aloud in the House of Commons, that a copy was presented to every member of Parliament, and that one was brought to the approving attention of Queen Victoria.

There is less argument about the facts of the *Journal's* success in America. It appeared the same month that Negroes were being lynched in the draft riots in New York. If the tide had already turned, those who had been breasting it for two and a half years did not know it yet. Some of them felt that Fanny's testimony was so valuable that it needed the widest possible circulation. The *Journal* was excerpted and circulated in pamphlet form all over the North, and there was still such a demand for the original version that Harper and Brothers ordered a second printing early in 1864.

Fanny had struck her blow at what looked to her like the blackest hour and had earned her right to the dawn that came after it. That glow was to warm the rest of her long life.

For there were no more agonizing decisions. She learned now to co-exist lovingly with those whose views and values were different from hers. Little by little she was reconciled with Fan, and the years of her grandmotherhood were as golden as those of her motherhood had been grim.

She was always a welcome guest in the Wisters' Philadelphia home, and she was devoted to her grandson, also named Owen, in whom she correctly saw a writer of promise. But as she grew old, Fanny was happiest in England. And it was with Fan that she found the contentment she wanted for her last years. For Fan was married to James Leigh, an English clergyman who had "come into the living" at Stratford on Avon. In Shakespeare's country Fanny found peace, close by her one unblemished love, "that greatest and best English mind and heart" in whose presence she had spent the best hours of her long life. On January 15, 1893, at the age of eighty-three, she died.

Janet Stevenson, whose article on the Grimké sisters appeared in our April, 1967, issue, has published several historical novels, including The Ardent Years, *which dealt with Frances Kemble Butler. Mrs. Butler's famous* Journal of a Residence on a Georgian Plantation in 1838–39, *edited by John A. Scott, was republished in 1961 by Alfred A. Knopf.*

READING, WRITING, AND HISTORY

By BRUCE CATTON

Imagination and History

Sometimes a quiet book about high and far-off times of long ago takes on disturbing overtones; as if, while he follows the story of things past, the reader begins to hear a faint but insistent cry from the street outside the window—a newsboy, perhaps, crying an extra, saying that something ominous is going on even though his words cannot at first be made out. Reading about a terror that vanished generations ago, we find it taking shape beside the armchair.

For an example of this, read William Irwin Thompson's thoughtful little book, *The Imagination of an Insurrection: Dublin, Easter 1916.*

In a way, this is a book of literary criticism. It is also a sketch of the famous Easter uprising in Dublin, which was quickly suppressed with shootings and hangings but which somehow touched off something that could never be suppressed. Most of all, the book is a study of the place of imagination in the making and understanding of history.

The thesis here is that a great historic happening cannot be understood without imagination. It could not even have taken place if someone's imagination had not been at work. What is and what is dreamed interact endlessly. As Mr. Thompson remarks: "History is, in fact, a process by which a private imagination becomes a public event, but any study that restricted itself to public events would have to ignore the fact that history is also the process by which

public events become private imaginations."

The Easter uprising of course had complex origins, but Mr. Thompson believes that it would not have come when and as it did if it had not been for the Irish literary renaissance of the early years of the century. The literary people were objecting to the increasing Anglicization of the land, which was eroding old traditions and old values, and to the increasing burden of raw industrialism—Dublin by 1916 had the worst slums in western Europe; and they were calling their countrymen's attention to a simpler, cleaner, more inspiring life of the past. They had no intention of creating an actual revolution, complete with bloodshed, wrecked buildings, and scaffolds. William Butler Yeats, the chief figure in the literary movement, whose play *Cathleen ni Houlihan* did so much to inspire the people who presently led the nationalistic movement, seems to have been slightly appalled by what he had helped to start. Years afterward he wrote a few lines of verse about it:

> *All that I have said and done*
> *Now that I am old and ill*
> *Turns into a question till*
> *I lie awake night after night,*
> *And never get the answers right.*
> *Did that play of mine send out*
> *Certain men the English shot?*

It did. Out of the imagination of writers complaining about their alienation from the society in which they lived came, in due time, one of these public events that derive from things imagined.

The Easter uprising, to be sure, was most amateurishly organized and executed, and it was quickly put down by British troops. It involved only a small minority of the people of Dublin, the authorities shot and clubbed it into extinction without great difficulty, and much of the disorder came because the mass of the slum dwellers, caring nothing about the uprising itself, went out into the streets to loot and pillage . . . and it is at this point that the reader begins to hear that distant and disturbing cry from the streets; have we not, in our own land and time, seen something rather similar happening?

Mr. Thompson sharpens it, step by step. He remarks that "from the beginning the Irish artist was placed in that psychologically painful situation which the American Negro writer now encounters," finding that

---

The Imagination of an Insurrection: Dublin, Easter 1916, by William Irwin Thompson. Oxford University Press. 262 pp. $6.75.

---

his real audience is not his own downtrodden people but the educated classes in power. These are not really the people he set out to talk to, and yet in the end they help him, because revolution is so often "the dream of those insecurely placed people at the bottom of the top and the top of the bottom"; the word filters down, and what started as an ideological movement begins at last to crystallize into an action program. Men start to think on a different level and in a different way, as witness the angry complaint of the nationalistic Irish labor leader James Connolly:

Ireland is rotten with slums, a legacy of Empire. The debt of this war will prevent us from getting money to replace them with sound, clean, healthy homes. Every big gun fired in the Dardanelles fired away at every shot the cost of building a home for a working class family. Ireland has the most inefficient educational system, and the poorest schools in Europe. Empire counsels us to pay pounds for blowing out the brains of others for every farthing it allows us with which to train our own.

It sounds familiar, somehow.

In any case, the Easter uprising eventually became one of those public events that set imaginations to work. The uprising was the work of poets—chief among them the heroic Padraic Pearse, who died on the scaffold for his pains; and "the imagination of the poet-rebels had been so far beyond the reality of the nation that it took the nation three years to catch up." Catch up it finally did, however, and before long a hard realist named Michael Collins took over and began the task of dismantling the British Empire. Collins indulged in no poetic flights and struck no heroic attitudes; he simply set out to bring about a

general state of disorder, betting that this would be more than the heavy-handed authorities could handle. He lost his life doing it, but he succeeded in what he tried to do. The empire began to shrink.

Mr. Thompson sees a pattern in all of this, and as he traces it, that disturbing cry from outside the window begins to come in more clearly. "Whether," he writes, "it is the case of the Jews rejecting the Egyptian Empire, the Irish rejecting the British Empire, the Black Muslims rejecting America, or . . . the Africans rejecting the entire civilization of the West, the pattern is similar. In the face of overwhelming material evidence of the superiority of one culture over another, the inferior culture elaborates a new myth in which it claims to possess the secret to a more holy, more moral, or more beautiful way of life." The intellectuals begin it, but somewhere along the line they meet ordinary folk who have wrongs that need to be righted: "The explosive power of revolution comes from this encounter of the intellectual trying to save his soul with the common man trying to get even as well as equal."

Furthermore, the explosion comes when we are not really looking for it—even when we think that things are at last beginning to get better. Hear Mr. Thompson on this point:

The revolution comes not when oppression is greatest, but when oppression has been relieved somewhat; it comes when the revolutionary can glimpse his chance and has the energy to seize it. The revolution came in Ireland when the farmers were profiting, as agricultural countries always do, from the war; it came when the farm boys, who were not bothered by conscription, were jealous of the heroes of 1916 and were looking for trouble. And even our own American Negro Revolution did not come when oppression was greatest, when the slightest mumble of complaint would bring instantaneous murder; it came at a time of improvement, when prosperity dramatized what the Negroes did not have, and liberal whites were displaying the symptom that Professor Brinton calls the failure in confidence of the ruling elite. The appearance of conscience and a divided consciousness in the men at the top is a signal for the men at the bottom, who by force of adversity are not troubled by such problems, to strike for their rights.

The intellectual, in short, starts something and then gets left behind by it, and Mr. Thompson points out that the Negro revolution, like the Irish, has its literary movement:

The early Yeats . . . screamed revolution, and was welcomed into the better salons of British power and was thus rendered harmless as a revolutionary. James Baldwin, shouting execrations and anathema, is welcomed into the best Manhattan penthouses, where his hands are politely tied by having an ash tray placed in one hand and a martini in the other. If history is always new in content and texture, it can repeat itself in form and structure.

From Dublin to Watts

It depends on whose imagination is being touched. History does not really contain any inevitabilities. It is just full of booby traps for the stupid. British imagination in 1916 could think of nothing for a Padraic Pearse except the hangman's noose; a few years later, it could think of nothing for Michael Collins but the Black and Tans; and today, as a partial but inescapable result, there is no British Empire. We still have a chance, over here, if we have enough imagination to see how to grasp it.

There was Dublin in 1916, and there was Watts in 1965, with fire in the streets, guns going off, and men being killed. An uncommonly gifted and perceptive writer named Budd Schulberg saw it all on television —the thing does have its uses, now and then—and had enough imagination to see that it compelled him as a writer to try to find out just what was going on in his own corner of the country. He came up with, at last, the most improbable answer you could think of. He went down into Watts, found an empty room amid the ruins, and opened a free school for writers.

He had quite a time, and he tells about it in one of the most moving books we are likely to get for a long time—*From the Ashes: Voices of Watts.*

To begin with, he narrowly escaped getting his head bashed in, the people in Watts being somewhat suspicious of outsiders. For another thing, he sat in his new school for weeks without getting a single applicant. For a third, he concluded that he might stir up a little interest by running the excellent movie *On the Waterfront,* for which he had written the script, and he asked if some neighborhood movie house could not put it on, for free—only to learn that there was not a movie house anywhere in Watts. He finally ran the

---

From the Ashes: Voices of Watts, edited and with an introduction by Budd Schulberg. New American Library. 275 pp. $5.95.

---

thing off for an audience of some thirty restless young bloods in a vacant storeroom, only to see the audience walk out on him halfway through because there was a boiling commotion at the undertaking establishment across the street. A woman had just brought in her dead six-months-old daughter, who would not have died if she could have been taken to a hospital quickly; the trouble was that there was no hospital within twelve miles. People were a little upset.

Running a writers' school under such circumstances could be difficult, but Mr. Schulberg kept at it.

He then discovered a thing that Eric Hoffer pointed to in *The Temper of Our Time*—namely, that this country "is simply lumpy with talent." Here he was, working in an area full of grade-school and high-school dropouts, dope addicts, young people with long police records, people down below the bottom of the ladder, and he got them writing and learned that they had something to say and, with a little help, knew how to say it. His book, *From the Ashes,* is a collection of stories, poems, and essays these Watts folk wrote, and their level is extraordinarily high.

It was not easy going. There was a young painter who burst out with the words: "Why fool around with a lot of fancy words for what we want? We all know what we want—freedom. It's the one word. Without freedom we aren't alive. We're walking dead men." And there was a self-taught musician who told him: "What's the use of writing what we want? We've been trying to say what we want for years, but who listens to us? We're not people. If you really thought we were human beings you wouldn't allow us to live like this."

However, Mr. Schulberg kept at it, and he got somewhere. He put people to work, and surprisingly often he uncovered work that deserved an audience. And as he did this he thought of the occasional individual who can speak for the many, and he writes of this man: "His single candle may light a thousand thousand candles. And the light and warmth of these candles may help redeem and regenerate the core of the ghetto, that decomposed inner city, waiting either for a phoenix to rise from the ashes or for bigger and more terrible fires."

It all depends (to repeat) on whose imagination is touched. The British in Dublin in 1916 had imaginations impervious to outside stimuli, and they could think of nothing but the hangman, the rifle squads, and the cop with his heavy club. It seems that there can be another way. Mr. Schulberg's book is one of the most hopeful indications in a long time, and it has nothing at all to do with the use of force.

What did Mr. Schulberg's people write? There is no space here to quote properly, but one sample may be meaningful. It is a poem called "Negro History," by Jimmie Sherman, and it goes like this:

> *A ship*
> *A chain*
> *A distant land*
> *A whip*
> *A pain*
> *A white man's hand*
> *A sack*
> *A field*
> *Of cotton balls—*
> *The only things*
> *Grandpa recalls.*

Among the Clouds

CONTINUED FROM PAGE 59

summit of Mount Washington at seven gallons a minute at a pressure of 2,000 pounds to the square inch.

The cog railway had a maintenance problem: the twelve-tooth pinion gears keyed to the two crankshafts of each locomotive frequently required replacement because of the heavy strains involved in running. Arthur Teague redesigned the assembly so that now shaft and gear are made from a single piece of chrome molybdenum steel.

By no means devoid of sentiment, Arthur Teague artfully restored an 1875 coach to its Victorian grandeur and equipped it with modern roller bearings. On the other hand, needing more and larger passenger cars, he designed coaches built from stock-size steel and aluminum sheets, thus reducing the price of the finished cars.

In one instance, Arthur Teague took a negative rather than a positive approach. In 1946, General Electric offered to build three diesel locomotives for the cog railway at $100,000 apiece, but Teague rejected the proposal, reasoning that the season was too short to permit the line to carry such a heavy debt. Today, twenty-two years later, the cog railway's six steam engines are a major attraction in themselves.

Their appeal is, of course, their rarity in a diesel age, yet that rarity poses problems. The cog railway's machine shop is required to do every imaginable job called for in keeping the six extant engines running: making and installing new boiler tubes, sidesheets, and flues; machining bearings; and making new crank and main shafts and its own patterns for outside casting.

Arthur Teague died last August. Almost as if this were an ill omen, tragedy struck the Mount Washington Cog Railway a month later. On September 17, 1967, a train carrying some eighty tourists was backing down the mountain in its usual lazy fashion when it ran into a mistakenly opened switch about a mile from the summit. The engine jumped the track; the coach, with nothing to hold it back, plunged on down the mountain another 500 feet and then bounced off the trestle, turning over as it did so and crushing eight passengers to death. Many others were injured.

While the accident—the only one involving passengers in ninety-eight years of service—has naturally cast a temporary pall over the cog railway, there is every indication that it will survive this worst blow in its history. The New Hampshire Public Utilities Commission has reported that "the primary cause of the accident was human error and not . . . any structural or mechanical deficiency of the railroad." Mrs. Arthur Teague has bravely announced her intention to carry on her husband's work, and full service to the summit of Mount Washington is positively expected to resume in the spring of 1968, as it has every spring since 1869. New safety measures, however, will be in effect.

A trip on the cog railway will remain as unusual and exciting as it has always been. Expectant crowds will wait for each train, will eye the steeply sloping track with awe, will crowd closely around the locomotives. Still a tradition will be the ticket-collecting stop on Jacob's Ladder; because of the 37.5 per cent grade, passengers at the front of the car are thirteen feet higher than passengers seated at the rear. Buildings beside the track, actually level, appear crazily tilted. So does the world that moves past the windows and the tilted seats in the coach. As the train ascends, the red spruce trees of the Base Station are soon replaced by wiry evergreens that diminish to twisted shrubbery at the timber line. Above the timber line is an Arctic world, the legacy of the long-gone glaciers. The train moves across a gray lunar landscape, its barrenness relieved only by the scenic panoramas that stretch for miles away from the heights. If the mountain is in a benevolent mood, travellers can see no fewer than seventy-four bodies of water, from the Atlantic Ocean to the Connecticut River. Visible from the summit on a clear day are the Adirondack Mountains of distant New York, the nearer peaks of Vermont's Green Mountains, and Mount Washington's neighbors in the Presidential Range. Portland, Maine; Laconia and Portsmouth, New Hampshire; and innumerable smaller towns are all in view.

Surprisingly, the trip up the mountain is a quiet one. For all their herculean labors, the six engines of the cog railway are mild of voice; their exhaust is a series of gentle chuffs rather than a staccato of explosive blasts. For children, each is The Little Engine That Could, come to life, its muted exhaust surely saying, "I-think-I-can, I-think-I-can," as it climbs New England's highest mountain. Ahead of it in the coach will be another three or four score riders who will agree, as thousands have before them, with P. T. Barnum's comment on the view from the top of Mount Washington: "The second greatest show on earth."

Mr. Ackerman, who is Sunday editor of the New Bedford, Massachusetts, Standard-Times, *is a long-time railroad buff, as well as "the only man who ever sailed backward up the Wareham River."*

Little Giant

Mount Washington ranks high among America's most popular peaks, even though there are scores of others (nearly all of them in the West) that are far higher in altitude. Its New England location, its ease of ascent, and the stunning view from its top have given it a longer and fuller history than perhaps any other lofty American mountain. Today its most learned chronicler is Frank Allen Burt, of Brookline, Massachusetts. Grandson of the man who in 1877 started *Among the Clouds,* the daily summer newspaper published at the summit for thirty-one years, Mr. Burt has gathered all of his Mount Washington lore into an absorbing book, *The Story of Mount Washington,* published by Dartmouth Publications in 1960. AMERICAN HERITAGE is grateful to him for the use of his book as a basic source for the accompanying article on the cog railway, and for the compilation of the following sampler of Mount Washington history.

Long a playground for tourists, hikers, and skiers, Mount Washington in the last century has also been an important natural laboratory for the study of cold-weather phenomena. Despite its generally delightful weather in other seasons—though there are sometimes sudden snow squalls even in summer—winter brings the mountain summit a climate more closely approximating polar conditions than any other equally accessible spot in the world. Winds blowing above 150 miles per hour are no surprise, while the thermometer quite casually drops to forty degrees below zero. This makes it something of a paradox that the mountain has, besides the cog railway, a good auto road to the top, and for many years boasted a large, comfortable hotel, the Summit House, that entertained thousands of happy summer visitors who were scarcely mountaineers. More distinguished Americans have probably ascended Mount Washington than any other mountain anywhere, not excluding Pikes Peak.

Here is a somewhat capricious selection of Mount Washington's notable events across three and a quarter centuries: **1642:** Darby Field, of Massachusetts Bay Colony, made the first ascent by a white man. **1784:** The Reverend Jeremy Belknap, D.D., climbed the mountain, named it Mount Washington, and estimated its height as above ten thousand feet (it actually measures 6,288). **1821:** Three young ladies from Jefferson, New Hampshire, were the first females to climb the mountain. **1849:** An English hiker named Frederick Strickland became the first of some thirty-five persons to die from exposure or climbing accidents on the slopes of Mount Washington during the last 119 years. **1855:** A. S. Walker of Boston walked to the summit barefoot. **1861:** The eight-mile carriage road (later called the auto road) was completed to the summit. **1869:** The cog railway was finished and began regular service. **1874:** The U.S. Army set up a weather station for winter observations at the summit which was operated regularly until 1887. **1873:** The Summit House (over a hundred beds) was built. **1877:** *Among the Clouds,* a daily summer newspaper, began publication. The same year, the first of several marriage ceremonies was performed at the summit. **1887:** Charlie O'Hara, stage driver, drove a carriage-and-six to the mountain top in one hour and nine minutes, and was then arrested for cruelty to animals. **1892:** A huge electric beacon, visible a hundred miles away, shone briefly from the summit to prove the power of the dynamo. **1899:** Freelan Stanley made the first motor ascent of the mountain, in his Stanley Steamer. **1900–07:** After arduous liquid training at the summit, Edgar Welch of Hiram, Maine, ran eight miles down the carriage road every year, wearing a tall beaver hat and endeavoring to beat his own record of forty-five minutes. **1908:** The Summit House burned down. **1932:** Mrs. Florence Clark drove her team of Eskimo dogs to the top singlehanded, just for the sport of it. **1934:** Wind velocity of 231 miles per hour was measured—the highest ever recorded anywhere. **1937:** An experimental FM radio station began broadcasting from the summit. **1939:** Toni Matt, skier, "schussed" (came straight down) the headwall of Tuckerman Ravine, a fifty-degree, thousand-foot snow bowl near the summit. **1942:** The U.S. government began tests—which are still going on—of cold weather equipment.

The Army Signal Service men who wintered atop Mount Washington to take weather observations in the 70's and 80's might as well have been in the Arctic.

Hugo Black and the K.K.K. CONTINUED FROM PAGE 64

dissenter being Republican Senator Warren R. Austin of Vermont, who raised a constitutional point. The authors of the Constitution, Austin argued, had forbidden a senator or representative to take a civil office that had been created or for which the salary had been increased during his term in Congress. Hugo Black was ineligible, this group contended, because he was a senator when an act was passed entitling Supreme Court justices to full pay after their retirement. Moreover, Justice Van Devanter had not resigned but only retired from active service; Austin and others insisted that Black would be filling a newly created post as the "tenth justice." Supporters of the administration replied pointedly that no such objections had been raised when the Senate had previously urged Roosevelt to name Senator Robinson to the court.

On Monday, August 16, the full Judiciary Committee held a stormy hearing, closed to the public and the press. Reporters wrote afterward that tempers "flared to a white heat" and two members had to be restrained from a fist fight.

The Klan issue had been broached by the National Association for the Advancement of Colored People and by the Public Affairs Committee of the Socialist party in telegrams asking for an investigation of Black's Klan relationship. Norman Thomas, chairman of the Socialist group, wanted the Senate also to explore Black's silence on the famous Scottsboro case and his opposition to antilynching bills. But such calls were quietly ignored. Without raising the Klan issue and despite Republican cries of "steamroller," the committee voted 13 to 4 to report the nomination favorably to the Senate.

Anticipating a floor fight, spectators packed the Senate galleries the next day. It was Senator Royal S. Copeland, a New Deal opponent and a candidate for mayor of New York City, who brought the rumors into the open. He read a 1926 report from the *New York Times* to the effect that Black, to win Alabama votes in the closing days of his first Senate race, had attacked the presidential aspirations of Governor Alfred E. Smith, a Catholic. Black's supporters were quick to reply that Democrat Copeland was now attacking Black to gain the votes of New York's Negroes and Catholics for his own mayoral candidacy. Senator Edward R. Burke, Democrat of Nebraska,

volunteered to produce in Washington two witnesses who, he said, had been present when Black was initiated into the Klan, but no one moved to take up his offer. Burke and Copeland urged the Senate to ask Black himself for a statement, but without success. In Atlanta, reporters sought out the Imperial Wizard of the Klan, Hiram W. Evans, who said that so far as he knew Black was neither a Klansman nor a sympathizer. "I'm hoeing my own row," he said.

While Black awaited the outcome in an office near the Senate chamber, a group of his colleagues reportedly called upon him and actually put the question. Black, by one account, replied that he was not presently a Klansman but added that if anyone was concerned lest he might have been a Klansman in the past, that man should vote against confirmation.

After this conversation, William E. Borah, Republican of Idaho, the old "irreconcilable," made the only statement in Black's behalf on the Klan question. "There has never been at any time one iota of evidence that Senator Black was a member of the Klan," Borah told his colleagues. He said that Black, in private discussion before the nomination, had stated that he was not a member of the Klan. No one, Borah said, had suggested any source from which evidence might be obtained. For himself, the Idaho senator said he would vote against any man whom he knew to be a member of a secret organization of the nature of the Klan. These remarks would come back to plague Borah.

After six hours of debate, administration lines held firm, and Senate traditions carried the day. A motion to send the nomination back to committee was defeated, and the Senate voted 63 to 16 to confirm it. Recording the outcome in his diary, Secretary of the Interior Harold Ickes summed it all up: "So Hugo Black becomes a member of the Supreme Court of the United States, while the economic royalists fume and squirm, and the President rolls his tongue around in his cheek." Pleased with his ploy, Roosevelt invited his nominee to lunch two days after the Senate vote and presented him with the com-

The New York World-Telegram, *unconvinced by Justice Black's explanation on network radio of his former Klan status, titled this cartoon "A New Justice Robes Himself."*

World-Telegram, OCTOBER 4, 1937

mission of an associate justice. Leaving the White House with the cardboard cylinder under his arm, Black told reporters: "I suppose I said 'thank you.'" Asked when he would take the Supreme Court oath, he replied that he had no idea.

By custom the Chief Justice administered the general oath, the one taken by all public servants, to a new justice in the robing room on the day he appeared to assume his duties. A second "judicial oath," applying particularly to the court, was usually administered by the court clerk in the courtroom before a new justice ascended the bench.

Precedent (and his own statement) to the contrary, the new associate justice took both oaths late that same afternoon. The simple ceremony took place in the office of the secretary of the Senate, Edwin A. Halsey. The only person present besides Halsey and Black was Charles F. Pace, financial clerk of the Senate, who notarized a printed form from the Department of Justice containing both oaths. In the closing hours of a hectic session of Congress, the oath-taking ceremony was only briefly reported. Those who noted it at all probably assumed that Black had taken only the general oath.

Thus on August 19, seven days after his nomination was sent to the Senate, Hugo Black became a full-fledged member of the United States Supreme Court, entitled by the Constitution to hold office "during good behavior" for his lifetime. He ordered his judicial robes, received the initial installment of his $20,-000 annual salary, and left for his first trip to Europe. The court was in recess until October.

Early opinions of the new justice varied with the political leanings of those who expressed them. Herbert Hoover said the court was "one-ninth packed." Raymond Moley, the onetime "brain truster" who had broken with Roosevelt, said he couldn't remember a worse appointment. But labor leaders were enthusiastic, and a liberal magazine called it the most courageous nomination since Woodrow Wilson named Justice Louis Brandeis, the court's first Jew.

While Justice and Mrs. Black were abroad, an enterprising reporter, Ray Sprigle of the Pittsburgh *Post-Gazette*, assisted by a large expense account and private detectives, was in Alabama searching into Black's political past. Sprigle's inquiries led him to the former Grand Dragon of the Alabama Ku Klux Klan, James Esdale, recently disbarred from the practice of law in Alabama and by this time also estranged from the Klan. As evidence that Black had actually been a member, Esdale showed Sprigle the note of resignation. Handwritten and dated July 9, 1925, it read: "Dear Sir Klansman, Beg to tender you herewith my resignation as a member of the Knights

of the Ku Klux Klan, effective from this date on. Yours I.T.S.U.B. Hugo L. Black." In Klan parlance, the initials stood for "In the Sacred, Unfailing Bond."

Sprigle also wangled from Esdale's files a stenographic transcript of the proceedings of the 1926 Klorero at which Democratic nominees Black and Graves had spoken and had been presented with Klan "grand passports." The transcript contained the full text of Black's "thank you" speech to the Alabama Klan. "I realize," the future Supreme Court justice was quoted as saying, "that I was elected by men who believe in the principles that I have sought to advocate and which are the principles of this organization."

In a series of six syndicated articles which began on September 13, 1937, Sprigle dramatically displayed his evidence for the nation to read. Newspapers all over the country spread across their front pages Sprigle's sensational accusation that the new justice "is a member of the hooded brotherhood that for ten long, blood-drenched years ruled the Southland with lash and noose and torch." To justify this bold statement, Sprigle contended that the note of resignation was a deliberate ruse, designed to protect the Klan's political candidate from criticism by Catholic and Jewish voters and other anti-Klan forces. Furthermore, Sprigle claimed that by accepting the "grand passport," Black had, in effect, accepted life membership in the Klan.

"That the White House was stunned by the exposé," wrote one Washington observer, "is putting it mildly. From the President down, the inner circle was astounded and frightened." Roosevelt was described as angry and embarrassed, but when a Cabinet member urged the President to clear himself by saying that he would not have named Black if he had known of the Klan membership, Roosevelt refused. He would play for time, he said, and await public reaction.

The President confided to Ickes that it had never occurred to him to ask Black about any such connection. In his diary Ickes recorded that F. D. R., an open foe of the Klan since the Democratic convention of 1924, was now in the position of having either "deliberately or carelessly" named a Klan member to the Supreme Court. "There is no doubt that this incident is very bad for the President," Ickes wrote. "There has been nothing like it."

With Senator Burton K. Wheeler, Democrat of Montana, demanding a presidential investigation, Roosevelt reviewed his plight with Ickes and Borah. They agreed that Klan membership was not grounds for impeachment and that the President had no more right to investigate a member of the Supreme Court than to investigate a member of the Senate. Roosevelt suggested that Black make a statement after his return from Europe; if he cleared himself in the mind of the public, he should remain on the court.

On September 14, with interest in the Sprigle series running high, Roosevelt faced the press. The President denied that he had known of Black's membership in the Klan before nominating him. His brief No was so emphatic that one reporter described it as a categorical denial and another as a "terse negative."

Belatedly, reporters found that the two witnesses whom Senator Burke had offered to produce were both special assistants to Attorney General Cummings himself. One, Black's former law partner, William E. Fort, refused to comment. The other, Walter S. Brower, denied that he himself was a Klansman.

Vacationing senators were tracked down and asked whether they would have voted for Black if they had known of his former membership. Some said they had been "misled"; others passed it off as a "tempest in a teapot." Borah, with difficulty, attempted to clarify his original statement, declaring he had not meant to tell the Senate that Black had never been a Klansman, but simply that he was not a member now.

Hundreds of other Americans joined the furor. William Allen White now said Roosevelt had "dishonored" the high court, but Senator George W. Norris continued to insist that it was a "wonderfully good appointment." Ickes, confronted by the press, produced an embarrassed administration's most adroit counterthrust: "I really think the greatest expert on the Ku Klux Klan is [President] Hoover. I refer you to him. He accepted their support. Nobody criticized him." Critics of Roosevelt and the New Deal—cartoonists in particular—had a field day. The President was criticized for not having sought advice before the nomination, and Black was castigated for not revealing his Klan connection to Roosevelt or the Senate.

The new justice, *Newsweek* declared, must accept responsibility for his silence during the Senate debate "and for the private advice confidentially but freely passed around Senate cloakrooms that he had no actual Klan ties, however much he owed the Klan for his first nomination and election to the Senate." But the *Nation,* admitting that Black had been a political opportunist when he joined the Klan, drew a distinction between opportunism and bigotry. Black, it said, had had to fight his way up from the "ignorance and bigotry of the Southern masses" to national prominence with only rudimentary schooling and without benefit of the tradition either of western populism or of the New England Brahmin. The exposé, the *Nation* concluded, was an effort by "powerful oligarchical minorities," led by William Randolph Hearst, to destroy Black's usefulness on the bench and force

Roosevelt to abandon his fight to liberalize the judiciary. The *Christian Century* said those who raised the furor "do not fear Black the Klansman as much as they hate Black the Inquisitor."

Meanwhile, still in Europe, the central figure of the *cause célèbre* tried in vain to escape pursuing reporters. Tracked down in Paris, Justice and Mrs. Black moved to London, but found their hotel surrounded by newspapermen. London papers were filled with the Sprigle series, and thereby thousands of Britishers received their first knowledge of the Ku Klux Klan. There were many notable visitors in London that season after the coronation of King George VI, but the most attention was centered upon the Blacks.

Toughened by years of experience in courtrooms, political campaigns, and Senate debates, Black was accustomed to the glare of the limelight—to pressure, harsh criticism, and a constant entourage of reporters. But his sensitive wife, Josephine, found it a searing experience. When the Blacks were unexpectedly accosted by a newspaperman in a dim hotel corridor, she was badly frightened.

On September 20 Justice and Mrs. Black eluded reporters long enough to board the mail steamer *City of Norfolk,* bound for that out-of-the-way Virginia port. Their names were not on the passenger list, for they had originally planned to return to New York aboard the S. S. *Manhattan,* on which three United States senators and another Supreme Court justice, James C. McReynolds, would have been fellow passengers.

As the *City of Norfolk* made its way west, the Gallup Poll reported that fifty-nine per cent of the Americans whom it interviewed thought the Justice should resign if it were proved that he had been a Klan member. Roosevelt told another press conference that he knew only what he had read in the newspapers and that there was nothing to say until Justice Black returned. When the President left for an extended tour of western states, his critics charged that he was trying to avoid Black.

The reporters at the Norfolk pier found the Justice outwardly cheerful and unperturbed. Among them was Sprigle himself, conspicuous in his customary western-style hat. Justice Black said he appreciated "this great reception," and added only: "When I have any statement to make that's definite and final on any subject, I will make it in such a way that I cannot be misquoted, and that the nation can hear me."

During his European trip, Black had apparently decided to present his reply over the radio, which would assure him of a direct confrontation with the American people, one that could not be slanted by writers for opposition newspapers.

With the help of his brother-in-law and a close

friend, Black composed his speech. Three nationwide networks cleared thirty minutes of time on the evening of October 1 for an unprecedented address by a Supreme Court justice on a controversial topic. The listening audience was estimated to be second only to that which had heard Edward VIII renounce the throne of Great Britain a year earlier. "Black radio parties" were held in many homes, and a few fiery crosses burned on northern hillsides.

Black spoke from the living room of a friend's modest home in a Washington suburb. Several couples, the women in long evening gowns, sat in an adjoining dining room; about one hundred curious onlookers gathered outside. Seated before a cluster of microphones, Black showed no outward sign of nervousness, although Jim Farley said the Justice was in "as tough a spot as any man in public life has ever faced." The speech lasted only eleven minutes. In contrast to his vigorous Senate style, Black spoke deliberately, as if measuring each word. Press accounts mentioned his "soft Southern voice" and his "Alabama drawl."

Black said he was breaking Supreme Court precedent because this was an "extraordinary occasion." He condemned what he called a "concerted campaign" to revive prejudice and religious bigotry by trying to convince Americans that he was intolerant of minority groups. He affirmed his belief in the religious guarantees of the Bill of Rights and insisted that his Senate record refuted every implication of intolerance.

Then came the admission his audience was waiting for. "I did join the Klan," said Justice Black. "I never rejoined. What appeared then, or what appears now on the records of that organization, I do not know." He said he had never considered the "unsolicited card" as a "membership of any kind" in the Klan. "I never used it. I did not even keep it." Black said he had dropped the Klan before becoming a senator and had had nothing to do with it since. He told his audience he had many friends among Catholics, Jews, and Negroes. Concluding, the Justice declared firmly: ". . . my discussion of this question is closed."

On the following day, public opinion began to make itself heard. Newspapers opposed to the President almost universally criticized the speech, calling it "too damned clever" and "the plea of a man caught with the goods." Even the pro-administration New York *Post*, commenting on Black's claim to many Catholic, Jewish, and Negro friends, remarked acidly: "We might reply in kind that one of our best liberal friends was a Klansman but we still don't think he ought to be on the Supreme Court."

But the Montgomery, Alabama, *Advertiser,* once Black's foe, commented that his critics "do not give a hoot whether he was a Klansman or a Hottentot in 1925. They hate him because he was a Rooseveltian." John L. Lewis said the speech was "powerful and straightforward," but Norman Thomas regretted that Black had failed "openly and manfully" to repudiate the Klan. One of Black's friends told Farley that the Justice had decided that to repudiate the Klan would be "throwing down" many who had helped him in Alabama.

It was reported that Roosevelt, in Fort Lewis, Washington, 2,440 miles away from the White House, did not hear the speech because his car had no radio. But "the man in the street," to whom the speech had been aimed, was believed to have been favorably impressed. As the President told Farley: "It was a grand job. It did the trick. You just wait and see." Late in October, a national poll reported that only forty-four per cent of Americans still thought Black should resign.

Three days after the speech, Black made his first appearance on the Supreme Court. Chief Justice Charles Evans Hughes, whose own nomination had once been opposed by Senator Black, greeted the new member cordially in the robing room. With Hughes sat associate justices whose philosophies and decisions had been scathingly criticized by Senator Black. Before the court were two petitions that Justice Black be barred on the constitutional grounds raised in the Senate.

Perhaps to avoid the possibility of a sensational challenge in the open courtroom, Justice Black did not choose to repeat the judicial oath publicly. Since the new member had been confirmed and had already taken both his oaths, Chief Justice Hughes considered the matter closed and planned merely to take the protests under advisement.

In view of some three hundred spectators who packed the chamber, Justice Hugo La Fayette Black, his face inscrutable, ascended the steps and took his place on the high bench.

Virginia Van der Veer (Mrs. Lowell S. Hamilton), a member of the history department of the University of Alabama in Birmingham, is completing her doctoral dissertation on the Senate career of Hugo Black.

For further reading: The 168 Days, by Joseph Alsop and Turner Catledge (Doubleday, Doran, 1938), and Mr. Justice Black, by John P. Frank (Knopf, 1948).

ELDERMAN IN THE WASHINGTON *Post*

Easter Sunday, 1873